E-COMMERCE

E-COMMERCE

A Knowledge Base

Brian C. Satterlee

Writers Club Press

San Jose New York Lincoln Shanghai

E-COMMERCE
A Knowledge Base

Writers Club Press
an imprint of iUniverse.com, Inc.

For information address:
iUniverse.com, Inc.
5220 S 16th, Ste. 200
Lincoln, NE 68512
www.iuniverse.com

ISBN: 0-595-19371-4

Printed in the United States of America

For my wife, Anita Gregory Satterlee, with whom God has blessed me far beyond my dreams and imagination.

Contents

Foreword

The small group of computer scientists, in 1969 when developing the first computer network, probably did not realize they were changing history. Their only goal at that time was to build a network that would allow researchers around the country to share ideas. The project was called ARPANET after the agency that paid for it–ARPA, the Department of Defense's Advanced Research Project Agency. They were successful in accomplishing their goal, however, the costs were enormous. Most of these people were highly technical and did not see any outside use for such a system. The first message handled from one university to another has been lost in history, but they were united by technology, and by the work of these dedicated peoples' accomplishments, world communication was created.

As with any high level technology, the uses become more diversified than what the original design intended it to do. Electronic mail started on this costly network. Also, heated political electronic debates on various subjects quickly ensued. One debate documented was directed toward a computer game called Space War. Again, this was poor use of a costly system; however, over the next decade the development of several small powerful personal computers made the desire to communicate the supreme importance at a cheaper cost. The development by the National Science Foundation of a network called NSFNET, which replaced the ARPANET, then became the backbone for today's Internet. The world was now connected.

The sharing of computer resources was still the goal for this new technology. A national presentation made in 1974 first brought to light the multiple uses of this new technology. In the presentation it was revealed that students would learn at home by computer and class interaction, families would do their banking by computer networking, families would order their groceries, etc, by computer networking, newspapers and other reading materials would be delivered by network, library access would be done at home, games would be played with people all over the country by network, television would be distributed by this computer network, and video communications would be done through this technology. This presentation received a great amount criticism by many that said this would never happen. History has proven them wrong, however.

Only the visionary truly saw the potential of this Internet for establishing E-Commerce. Perhaps, the first real E-Commerce was done at Stanford University when researchers on the fourth floor sent a message through the Internet to check to see if there were soft drinks in a machine on the first floor. They had wired the machine to check for inventory before running down stairs to make a purchase. As redundant as this sounds, the ability to establish connection to other sites and various companies for products and services through the Internet has now created a whole new business direction.

E-Commerce has been said by many to have revitalized the American dream. Newly formed companies have created web sites that are accessible by millions. The success and failures of E-Commerce can be paralleled with the auto industry in its forming years. There were so many car manufacturers that their names when totaled went through the alphabet three times. The question is where are they now? Poor planning, poor decision making, poor design, poor leadership, provincial thinking, etc. all contributed to their demise. The same has recently occurred with several Internet companies because of similar problems. In any capitalistic country E-Commerce is expected to grow and grow logarithmically, however, there are many new techniques needed for true success that do differ from the older traditional approaches. These new techniques are a taught technology and not something one just has in their normal ways of thinking. Because of Internet's world link, globalization thinking is the top priority, as well as developing many new operational thinking techniques before actually doing or creating business in the electronic environment. The following pages of this text provide the contemporary information for doing business in this highly revolving medium.

With the world population now owning or having access to a computer, the method of doing business will be changing drastically in the future years. The methods of doing business through E-Commerce will be as different as the change between human labor and automation in the manufacturing industry was in the 1980s. It is, therefore, imperative that modern business people develop an understanding of these new processes.

Dr. Lloyd Thompson
Professor
June 2001

Acknowledgements

My graduate-level students contributed significantly to this project through their course participation and their reports on organizations in which they worked and conducted research. Special acknowledgement is given to Charles Bowman, Michelle Papierniack, Philip Parker, and Donnie Wilkerson.

Introduction

Electronic Commerce is one of the most important aspects to emerge from the Internet. It allows people to exchange goods and services immediately and with no barriers of time or distance. Any time of the day or night, one may go online and buy almost anything one desires. It has radically altered the macro-aspects of the economic and social environments. It has had great impact on large sectors of the economy, including communications, finance, and retail trade. It will engender massive changes in other areas, such as education, health, and government.

The combination of regulatory reform and technological innovation enabled E-Commerce to evolve into its present state. No doubt the precursor of the Internet was developed in the late 1960's—yet the arrival of the following innovations were major catalysts in the development of E-Commerce: the Information Super Highway; the development of the World Wide Web and browser technology; the liberalization of the telecommunications industry; and the expansion in the volume and capacity of communications technologies (optic fiber, digital subscriber line technologies, satellites, and the like).

Consequently, the barriers that once existed between buyers and sellers in terms of E-Commerce have progressively fallen. Initially, E-Commerce was primarily the domain of large firms, due to its initial format of customized, complex, and expensive transactions—essential barriers to entry by smaller competitors. Today, for a nominal fee, anyone may become an online merchant, with the potential to reach millions of consumers world-wide. This democratization of the Internet has changed the previous focus of E-Commerce from primarily Business-to-Business transactions between known parties, to a complex web of commercial activities involving huge numbers of consumers who never meet. In essence, the development of the Internet has had the same effect on E-

Commerce as Henry Ford's assembly line on the automotive industry. It has converted a luxury for the few into a relatively simple and inexpensive device for the masses.

In this book, we will explore these impacts and innovations. The purpose of this book is to provide a preliminary analytical foundation (knowledge base), which then may be used for further, more advanced study. It is not intended to be an exhaustive analysis—yet at the same time provides as much information as possible to provide an accurate depiction of the current state and likely future direction of E-Commerce.

The Knowledge Base

Many textbooks have been published in the various academic field of study. Some are written to meet the guidelines set forth by specialized accrediting agencies; others, to impart the results of research or scholarly activities. Whatever the reason for publication, all textbooks in their respective field of study cover their core concepts. A core concept in a given academic discipline is one that is central to the field. All scholars may not agree that it is "correct," yet it heavily influences their thinking (through acceptance, modification, or rejection) and is likely to stand the test of time. This book provides a knowledge base for the emerging field of E-Commerce, thus creating a framework for the core concepts of E-Commerce.

Tradition and the Internet

While business/management core concepts have stood the test of time, the application of these concepts to the professional situations of the student is in a constant state of change. How do business schools attempt to accommodate this constant state of change? Current instructional practice in most business schools is to present the core concept via an established textbook and require students to demonstrate competency in the concept by conducting a case analysis or some other experiential activity. The case study assignment requires the student to assess the situation as presented in the case, consider this assessment in light of the core concept(s) studied, and develop solutions for the case that are based on the core concept(s). In the end, students learn to apply traditional textbook-based concepts to traditional problems. Yet, as has been reported in the media, "the Internet has changed everything."

Has the Internet changed the relevancy of business/management core concepts? The assumption of this book is that the relevancy of the time-tested core concepts has not changed. What the Internet has changed is access to these core concepts. It is now possible for anyone to learn the core concepts of business, or any other field of study, via the Internet. This real-time access to information can be used to revolutionize the application of core concepts to the professional lives of those who learn them.

Limitation and Solution for Structuring Knowledge

While the Internet has revolutionized access to this knowledge base, it provides no method or process for structuring this information. Thus, the information remains as is–facts and figures. When meaning and structure are added to information, knowledge is produced. Whereas the traditional textbook adds value to the learner by providing a structure to the knowledge, no such provision exists for the Internet. The purpose of this book is to provide a knowledge base structure for the Internet-based study of E-Commerce.

Unique Learning Approach Used in This Book

Research on the known Internet information outlets has shown that current E-Commerce information can be fragmented, out of date, and hard to find. It was decided that the best way to approach this problem was not to try to present an extended discussion of the information itself, but to direct the prospective enquirers to a source of the required information—that is, the elements of the knowledge base. In essence, this book provides a short, sharp "mini-directory" of where one may learn more and structure their knowledge of E-Commerce. A primary advantage of the Internet is the array of information outlets available to users. In this book, each element of the knowledge base is supported by links to Websites that provide the most current information available for that topic. The questions at the end of each chapter are related to these sites, and should help the reader structure their knowledge with efficiency and purpose. Opportunities to investigate the core concept in greater depth can be realized by following the links provided from the various Websites (for each chapter).

Selection of Knowledge Base URLs

Each knowledge base Website was selected strictly for its intellectual content. Information on the Internet exists on a continuum of reliability and quality. It has been said, "knowledge is power." In the virtual environment of the Internet, only some information is power–reliable information. Source evaluation, defined as the determination of information quality, requires the use of multiple indicators to ensure quality and reliability. The indicators used to evaluate the Websites referenced in this text are: credibility (an authoritative source that supplies good evidence that allows you to trust it); accuracy (a source that is correct today–not yesterday–and gives a balanced perspective of the topic); reasonableness (engages the core concept thoughtfully and reasonably, concerned with the truth); and support (provides convincing evidence for the claims made, a source one may triangulate).

Suggestions for Internet-Based Learning

The Internet, then, is in a continual state of change and revision. Keeping up with this change can be very challenging. Fortunately, the Internet allows easy access to many of the sources needed to remain on the cutting edge of the E-Commerce knowledge base . The following suggestions are provided to help the reader cope with Internet-based learning:

Understand that it is the nature of Websites to constantly change. Revisions and deletions occur daily, and sometimes the actual URL changes. Be ready to accommodate for these changes.

Sometimes one may receive an error message such as, *"There was no response. Server could be down. Try later."* The usual culprit in these instances: too many users trying to log on at the same time. When this happens, attempt to log on again. If this doesn't work, try 20 minutes later. You should be able to eventually login the site.

If you receive a message that the Website does not exist, try entering the URL again but omit some of the last part, i.e., enter the home address only. Once in the Website, locate the desired destination via the Site Map.

What To Do In The Event A Knowledge Base Website Is No Longer Available

Refer to the chapter heading that corresponds to the knowledge base element, then use that chapter heading as a descriptor (for your favorite Search Engine) to find other sources for the particular element. For example, suppose the URL linking you to the topic heading, *Distribution,* is no longer active. Access a Search Engine of your choice, insert the topic heading, and search for new sites related to that heading. Be sure to employ the four criteria for source evaluation when selecting replacement URLs: credibility, accuracy, reasonableness, and support.

How To Use This Book

This book can be used by anyone interested in using the Internet to gain or improve or structure their knowledge of E-Commerce: the business practitioner, the business student, and the business school professor. Each chapter covers a specific element of E-Commerce, which in turn, is subdivided into three topical areas. A brief discussion of each element and topical area is provided, along with URL's that link the reader to further investigation via the Internet. Questions for review and knowledge testing are included at the end of each chapter.

CHAPTER 1:
DEFINING E-COMMERCE

The future is upon us. The Internet is expected to revolutionize society over the next 20 years as did the telephone in the early 1900s. The implications for business are staggering. Like the railroad, telephone, automobile and airplane, the Internet changes everything. We are headed for what William Knoke, author of *Bold New World: The Essential Road Map to the 21st Century*, calls the "placeless society" where communications portability makes location irrelevant. With geographic independence comes the economic irrelevance of the city, the factory, the office building—even the school and the household—each of which are defined in terms of place and proximity to other people. In the placeless society of the 21st century, it doesn't matter where you are. "It used to be that we had to have face-to-face contact," explains Knoke. "We had to have customer and supplier meet. We had to have retail stores to walk into. We had to come together in thirteen floors in a downtown office building to have a 'critical mass' to work together. But in the days of what I call 'connector technologies'—computers, telecommunications and transportation—we no longer need to 'physically' connect to interact."

What is E-Commerce?

http://www.internetpolicy.org/briefing/3_00.html

E-Commerce is defined as any transaction over the Internet involving the transfer of goods, services, or information, or any intermediary function that helps enable those transactions. This includes Business-to-Business E-Commerce, Business-to-Consumer E-Commerce, and information retrieval. E-Commerce engenders access to the Internet, including venues such as television and wireless devices such as Palm Pilots or personal data assistants, and personal computers

The most popular items sold via the Internet are tangible goods: computer products, books and magazines, music, and entertainment products. E-Commerce is quickly becoming a favorite way for both consumers and businesses to buy and sell products. Although a definite upward sloping trend line exists, it is difficult to predict an actual annual growth rate. The International Telecommunications Union estimated Business-to-Business E-Commerce in 2001-02 in a range from $100 billion to $400 billion, and Business-to-Consumer from $25 billion to $90 billion. Another estimate claims that E-Commerce is expected to grow to $707 billion in 2003. Internet sales could reach $115 billion annually by 2005.

What is known is that global E-Commerce in 1999 amounted to approximately $300 billion, about $250 billion of which took place in the United States. Even with this predicted growth, it is important to note that this is only a small percentage of total estimated retail sales. The Commerce Department estimated that retail E-Commerce sales accounted for $5.3 billion in the fourth quarter of 1999. While this may seem large, it is small compared to the total estimate of retail sales of $821 billion for the same quarter.

How to Start Selling Online

www.ecommercetimes.com/small_business
/getting_started/firstdata.shtml

Building an electronic store may appear to be a daunting task The ever-increasing array of E-Commerce products and services available contribute to this confusion. Building a strong foundation requires careful planning and a well-crafted strategy. Once it is determined which products and services lend themselves to selling online, five steps are essential in building the online store. With each step one may either complete the work individually or hire someone for assistance. Time and money are the two major factors to consider when deciding whether or not to hire a vendor that offers an integrated solution.

Step One: Domain Name Registration. A domain name is the company's location on the Internet. This name must be registered with the InterNic, an agency that registers and maintains a database of domain names. Although many providers that can help one obtain a domain name, often an Internet Service Provider (ISP) can provide this service.

Step Two: Web Store Design. The key decision to be made is whether to build or design the web page on your own, or hire a consultant to assist you. If one decides to hire a consultant, several issues must be addressed: what products and/or services that will be offered, the overall look of the site, the type of navigation tools to use, the forms of payment that will be used, as well as others. Once complete, the vendor can publish your site online.

Step Three: Server Hosting. It must be determined whether to buy a server and host your website in-house or outsource to a service provider. Hosting yourself can get complicated and may require several months to implement. However, outsourcing to a service provider can take only a few hours of time.

Step Four: Payment System. The following capabilities are required for selling online: payment software, a merchant account, payment processing services, and a gateway to connect all these items in the payment process. Cash register software is needed to calculate charges, and an account should be opened with a merchant bank. The merchant bank will retain the services of a payment processing company to handle transactions and place money into your account.

Step Five: Traffic Coverage. A business needs to let potential customers know that it is open for business. In order to accomplish this, the site must be registered with search engines. Registering includes determining key words, or descriptors, that will be associated with the site. Descriptors are what the search engines deploy in compiling searches. Another idea is to add the website to an online or virtual shopping mall.

As previously stated, a decision must be made, throughout the five steps, as to whether do the work yourself or outsource the work to some-one else. These steps may still appear to be complex and confusing, but one can always use an integrated solution. Companies such as First Data Merchant Services can handle each step and have the online store opera-tional in less than a day. Four variables affect this decision: (1) the amount of time available to create, run and update a site; (2) whether or not the cost of a consultant is supported in the budget; (3) the amount of expert-ise it takes to run a site effectively; and (4) how much control you want over your site (http://**www.senate.gov/~leahy/stepone.html**).

The costs to starting your **website** can vary widely. Forman Interactive offers Internet Creator for less than $150 (http://**builder.cnet.com/Business/Ecommerce20/ss04.html**).   Yahoo's Yahoo Store will host a site based on the number of items to be sold. The cost is $100/month for fifty items or less. The price then changes to $300/month for up to 1,000 items. Companies with a high volume of sales may pay from $10,000 to $100,000 or more. (It must be noted that this price is not the entire cost of running an E-Commerce site.) A low risk, low cost way of starting is to take advantage of the E-Commerce hosting services that are run by AT&T and MCI.

While the task of starting a website seems complex, there is much information available that can make this decision move forward smoothly. There are also many resources available to help one get started.

Technology Standards

http://www.bci1net.com/commerce.html/co00010.htm

Technological Standards on the Internet have rapidly changed over the past decade as new and faster technology has been employed by computer systems. In addition, software languages and codes have changed to meet the needs of customers' demand by using new computer speed access. These changes have developed a communication problem, as global communities attempt to link across the web. Thus, as businesses begin to use the web to reach new customers, a standard system is necessary to ensure that maximized return is generated on each hit to a web site. Today, there are few limitations on the standards in which a programmer may use in a software package. However, to maximize the return, the software should be as compatible with as many other computers as possible. These challenges address the need for a standard Internet code for global E-Commerce.

During the 1970's the first universal language, EDI, was developed. The government created EDI, Electronic Data Interchange, and several Fortune 1000 companies use this common language code. However, EDI requires an extensive private network and requires all communication to route through the exact same network. It does not allow for flexibility of different languages, network systems, or even web-based linkages.

Designers of EDI networks, to meet the demand of web browsers and Internet users, have developed a "store-front" image that can be accessed by other computers systems via the World Wide Web. The "store front" image does not require a direct EDI system. These "store front" systems use the universal code HTML, hypertext markup language. This universal language allows network and web browser users to access the same information by common codes. Large networks that utilize the EDI language, via linkages called junction boxes, can also allow for universal access. However, security clearances are needed to ensure that both parties are protected by these Universal codes.

HTML language codes also employ technology known as OBI, or Open Buying on the Internet. OBI is similar to the old EDI system, except OBI allows for open communication between non-networked computer systems. The advantage is that it introduces potential new customers to the system. However, this openness may create security problems, which must be address by encryption coding. Safeguards, such as (SSL) Secure Sockets Layer, (OPS) Open Profiling Standard, and (SET) Secure Electronic Transactions have all been developed to address the security issues. Each of these programming codes uses different encryption codes to protect both the buyer and the seller from loss of secure information and trust. Finally, a seal of approval, or **Truste,** can been added to websites. This seal ensures consumers of their privacy (to protect the World Wide Web from modern-age pirates).

Barriers to E-Commerce

http://www.commerce.net/research/research.html

A survey conducted by CommerceNet reported the following results: (1) some shoppers don't trust E-Commerce, (2) they can't find what they're looking for, and (3) there's no easy way to pay for things. Customers are worried about credit card theft, the privacy of their personal information, and unacceptable network performance. Some shoppers still aren't convinced that it is worthwhile to access the Internet, search for shopping sites, wait for the images to download, try to figure out the ordering process, and then worry about whether their credit card numbers will be pirated.

E-merchants will have to do a lot of educating to convince consumers that purchasing online is worth the effort. Gail Grant, the head of CommerceNet's financial research arm, predicts that most buyers will be won over in just a few years. Grant says that if Web pages were labeled with tags communicating product and pricing information, it would be easier for search engines to find items to buy online. That hasn't happened yet, she adds, because merchants want people to find their products, not their competitors'—especially if another company's goods are less expensive.

As for Business-to-Business systems, the issues are less emotional but still serious. Businesses do not yet have universal models for setting up their E-Commerce sites, and may have trouble sharing the orders and information collected online with the rest of their business applications. Many companies continue to grapple with the idea of sharing proprietary business information with customers and suppliers—an important component of many Business-to-Business E-Commerce systems. The key to solving this business model is for merchants to stop relying on Java applets (**www.irt.org/articles/js151/#java_applets**), and to restructure operations to take advantage of E-Commerce. Says Grant. "E-Commerce is just like any automation—it amplifies problems with their operation they already had."

QUESTIONS

1. What is E-Commerce? (**www.internetpolicy.org/briefing/3_00.html**)

2. What are the six characteristics that must be in place for E-Commerce to thrive? (**www.bci1net.com/commerce.html/co00010.htm**)

3. What do SET, OPS, and SSL stand for and why are they important for the use of E-Commerce?
(**www.bci1net.com/commerce.html/co00010.htm**)

4. What are the issues regarding business to business E-Commerce trans-actions? Are they different from direct to end consumer transactions? (**http://builder.cnet.com/Business/Ecommerce20/ss08.html**)

CHAPTER 2:
GLOBAL IMPLICATIONS

The Internet is opening up new venues for global commerce. This chapter covers The White House framework for global E-Commerce, resultant barriers that must be overcome, and the technology required to develop global E-Commerce.

Framework for Global E-Commerce

(http://www.ecommerce.gov/framewrk.htm)

No single force embodies the electronic transformation of society more than the evolving medium known as the Internet. It is changing classic business and economic paradigms. New models of commercial interaction are developing as businesses and consumers participate in the electronic marketplace and reap the resultant benefits. Entrepreneurs are able to start new businesses more easily, with smaller up-front investment requirements, by accessing the Internet's worldwide network of customers.

Commerce on the Internet totaled tens of billions of dollars by 2001. For this potential to be realized fully, governments must adopt a non-regulatory, market-oriented approach to electronic commerce—one that facilitates the emergence of a transparent and predictable legal environment to support global business and commerce. Official decision makers must respect the unique nature of the medium and recognize that widespread competition and increased consumer choice should be the defining features of the new digital marketplace. Governments can have a profound effect on the growth of commerce on the Internet. By their actions, they can facilitate electronic trade or inhibit it. Knowing when to act and—at least as important—when not to act, will be crucial to the continuous development of electronic commerce. The White House suggests the following principles for international discussions and agreements to facilitate the growth on the Internet.

The private sector should lead. Though government played a crucial role in financing the initial development of the Internet, its expansion has been driven primarily by the private sector. For electronic commerce to flourish, the private sector must continue to lead. Innovation, expanded services, broader participation, and lower prices will arise in a market-driven arena, not in an environment that operates as a regulated industry.

Governments should avoid undue restrictions on electronic commerce. Unnecessary regulation of commercial activities will distort development of the electronic marketplace by decreasing the supply and raising the cost of products and services for consumers the world over.

Where governmental involvement is needed, its aim should be to support and enforce a predictable, minimalist, consistent and simple legal environment for commerce. The goal should be to ensure competition, protect intellectual property and privacy, prevent fraud, foster transparency, support commercial transactions, and facilitate dispute resolution.

Governments should recognize the unique qualities of the Internet. The genius and explosive success of the Internet can be attributed in part to its decentralized nature and to its tradition of bottom-up governance. These same characteristics pose significant logistical and technological challenges to existing regulatory models, and governments should tailor their policies accordingly.

Electronic commerce over the Internet should be facilitated on a global basis. The Internet has emerged as a venue for the global marketplace. The legal framework supporting commercial transactions on the Internet should be governed by consistent principles across state, national, and international borders that lead to predictable results regardless of the jurisdiction in which a particular buyer or seller resides.

Barriers to Global Electronic Commerce

(http://www.oecd.org/dsti/sti/it/ec/prod/dismantl.htm)

Developments in global network technologies and graphic-based Internet applications make transmission of all kinds of digitized data fast, inexpensive and simple, at a time when public consumption of computer technologies is increasing. This environment offers lower barriers to entry for electronic commerce. By virtue of the Internet's architecture, electronic commerce was "born global", i.e., geographical and political boundaries mean little in this networked environment.

The intense interest in electronic commerce's economic impact is linked to the fundamental fact that it shrinks the economic distance between producers and consumers. Consumers can go directly to producers without the need for traditional retailers, wholesalers and, in the case of intangibles, distributors. While much media attention has focused on on-line merchants selling books, wine and computers to consumers, the available data suggest that the biggest E-Commerce market involves businesses supplying products to other businesses, where transactions of just a few firms exceed all estimates of the Business-to-Consumer market.

While the attributes of the Internet enable electronic commerce, they also hinder its growth for reasons as varied as: lack of trust, uncertainty about the regulatory environment, gaining access, and logistical problems for payment and delivery. Before users can engage in on-line commercial transactions, they must be able to access and use the network infrastructure. This includes access to information technologies such as computers, servers and software, as well as to the network itself, which is composed of a number of different infrastructures. Further hardware and software innovations are needed to create a wide variety of devices so that access is not a function of income, location, price, or specialized skills. Trust is central to any commercial transaction. Developing new kinds of commercial activities in the electronic environment largely hinges on assuring consumers and businesses that their use of network services is secure and reliable and that their transactions are safe.

More than Technology

(http://www.business2.com/content/magazine/ebusiness/1999/11/01/10693)

While the potential is undeniable, going global may be costly in the short run and much more complex than it appears. According to IDC, globalization is an imperative in the next wave of the Internet Economy. Howeer, most Web merchants are unaware of how to make it happen effectively. Anna Giraldo Kerr, senior analyst with IDC's Internet and E-Commerce Strategies Research Program, cautions that some U.S. sellers' enthusiasm for the Net may be blinding them. "They're saying 'Wow, we can receive orders from around the world 24 hours a day.' But then reality checks in and says 'How are you going to fill those orders?'" Giraldo Kerr explains basic sales strategies, such as first figuring out if there's a demand for your product, must still be adhered to in cyberspace. "That sometimes gets lost and blurry because we often equate E-Commerce just with technology," she says. Rather, she explains, globalization means establishing a presence in other countries with the help of the Internet.

Identifying a lucrative market outside the United States is only the first step. Discovering how to tap into it is another matter wrought with complex, often costly, tasks. To globalize, analysts assert, U.S. Internet firms must localize. This paradox implies many challenges. For one, companies must establish and implement warehousing and delivery infrastructures with a foreign country's currency, laws, and business modes in mind. And they need to translate, present, and maintain content that captures the nuance, subtleties, and tastes of another culture. Clearly, going global is not for those who view the world through U.S.-centric glasses. Even in countries where the same language is spoken, "translating" content is still a must when tailoring a Website to a particular culture. And this task is only one of many when it comes to implementing an effective global strategy.

Experts strongly recommend taking the partnering approach. "Taking the time to find the right partners is essential because they will open doors in the region as your ambassador," advises IDC's Giraldo Kerr. Partnering establishes an instant local presence, experts say, and consequently potential customers begin associating a brand with someone they know.

Questions

1. What are some barriers to E-Commerce?
(http://www.ecommerce.gov/framework.htm)

2. Consumer confidence in E-Commerce will require consumer protection mechanisms that address what four key issues?
(**http://www.oecd.org/dsti/sti/it/ec/prod/dismantl.htm**)

3. Explain the seven tips for globalization.
(**http://www.business2.com/content/magazine/ebusiness/1999/11/01/10693**)

CHAPTER 3:
LEGAL IMPLICATIONS

The U.S. Government remains heavily involved in business, through regulation, policies, and taxation. The growth of E-Commerce however, has changed the way that government interacts and regulates business. On one hand, many situations in E-Commerce are the same as in other forms of commerce, and there are already systems in place to handle this. On the other hand, E-Commerce is a totally new way of doing business and the legal implications are only beginning to be dealt with by government agencies, politicians, lawmakers, and judges. In the future, as E-Commerce continues to grow, the legal implication including government regulation, and most importantly, taxes, will become even more important. The one thing that is known is that the government will attempt to increase involvement in E-Commerce.

GOVERNMENT AGENCIES

www.nam.org/ECom/law/law.html

The government has, in times past, created bureaucracy to regulate uses of new technology. The Internet and the technology associated with it are no exception. Many of the legal issues concerning the Internet have been around for a long time and there are already government departments, committees and non-profit organizations to deal with these issues.

The Internet is impacted by the same problems affecting other media. The difference lies in the Internet's speed of information delivery and relatively inexpensive access. Still, the government is increasing involvement to regulate the Internet in the areas of domain name conflicts, false and deceptive acts on the Internet, and E-Commerce taxation.

The Internet Corporation for Assigned Names and Numbers (ICANN) manages the registration of domain names. It oversees and accredits registrar organizations to sell domain names on a first come/first served basis. It has set up procedures to resolve conflicts between trademark owners and organizations that use similar names in their domain names. It also resolves issues regarding multiple jurisdictions and foreign parties.

The Federal Trade Commission (FTC) has the responsibility of policing illegal activities on the Internet. This includes any unfair and deceptive acts that occur with online transactions. While the FTC does deal with some unusual problems regarding Internet transactions, many of the areas it regulates are similar to typical non-Internet transactions. For instance, the FTC ensures that advertisers and businesses have a reasonable basis for product claims before claims are made.

POLICIES, LAWS, AND REGULATIONS

http://www.ecommercetimes.com/news/articles/991117-2.shtml

Even though many laws associated with other media can be translated to the Internet, there are still many loopholes and problems that are peculiar to E-Commerce. Congress, the Federal Trade Commission and other regulating organizations have been slow to pass laws that deal solely with the Internet and its use. They have relied on laws governing other business practices to be transferred to this new media. Many argue that this is acceptable since E-Commerce is still, regardless of how glamorous, just a form of business. Laws that deal solely with the Internet and its use are either ill defined or non-existent. Similarly, the fast paced world of the Internet and E-Commerce is changing so quickly that laws may become obsolete soon after passage.

Some e-businesses are taking full advantage of the lack of legal standards in the area of E-Commerce, but many in the industry are lobbying for new laws, dealing strictly with E-Commerce, to be enacted. With so few laws dealing with E-Commerce, much of the discussion about new laws stems from laws applied to traditional "brick-and-mortar" business.

According to some experts (**www.inetstrategies.com/Legal.htm**), regulating the Internet is impossible because no single country, organization, or person owns the Internet. What complicates this is that every country has its own laws governing media and freedom of information. It is currently impossible to mesh the legion sovereign laws to effectively work in the Internet Age. This issue was exemplified in the Microsoft case. The case was based on antitrust laws enacted in the late 1800's, when industries such as steel and railroads dominated. Now high-speed computers and software dominate and no matter how much control a company may have, the industry and technology are evolving at an ever-increasing pace. According to some, even laws governing privacy, contract, even pornography may not effectively work in the new E-Commerce world.

One area in which questions have been raised is copyright law. How does one protect intellectual property, once it is placed on the Internet? The Digital Millennium Copyright Act prohibits anyone from tampering with any copyright management information. Still it is often hard to detect when intellectual property has been illegally copied.

Another major area of concern regarding E-Commerce and the Internet includes the gathering of data, information, and privacy laws. Currently the law protecting Internet privacy applies only to children. Many are concerned that employers and insurance agencies may have access to medical records. While the Department of Health and Human Services issued a statement regarding online medical records, Congress has not passed legislation dealing with this. As consumers conduct increased transactions on the Web, the government will be forced to intervene and regulate the Internet.

TAXATION

http://www.internetpolicy.org/briefing/april_00.html

Probably the most pressing legal concern of many regarding E-Commerce is taxation. "Brick-and-mortar" businesses want to know why the law requires them to pay sales taxes, property taxes and various licensing fees, while online organizations are required to pay none of these. State officials are concerned with the growth of Internet commerce and the potential loss of sales tax revenues. Both groups are lobbying heavily to levy sales tax on E-Commerce transactions. Local governments' estimate that $5 billion annually are already lost to out-of-state mail order business, and with the rapid rise of E-Commerce, this number will only increase. A number of states have reported declines in sales tax revenues. Many experts believe this is doubtful. Even with the huge growth in E-Commerce transactions, it is expected to be years before lost sales tax revenue becomes a serious problem.

Others argue that the tax-free status of online transactions has helped dramatically with the growth in E-Commerce. In 1998, Congress passed the Internet Tax Freedom Act placing a three-year moratorium on Internet taxes. This is likely to be extended into the future. The Act also set up an Advisory Commission on Electronic Commerce to study online taxation and related issues.

Ironically, what many people do not realize is that most transactions should have a sales tax levied. Organizations are required to collect state and local taxes from any buyer located within the organization's locality and state. If the organization is not in the same locality as the buyer, (as is the case with most Internet transactions) the buyer is supposed to pay to its jurisdiction a "compensation use" tax to compensate for the fact that no sales tax was collected. As no surprise, it is impossible to enforce these laws with the number or online transactions that occur.

QUESTIONS

1. When doing business on the Internet, what country's laws are you governed by? (**http://www.inetstrategies.com/Legal.html**)

2. What are the four broad policy options available regarding Internet sales taxes? (**http://www.internetpolicy.org/briefing/4_00_story.html**)

3. What are the arguments for and against developing laws specifically regarding E-Commerce?
(**www.ecommercetimes.com/news/articles/991117-2.shtml**)

CHAPTER 4:
ECONOMIC IMPACTS

The Internet has a dramatic effect on the economy. First, market prices for Internet stocks reached unheard of heights to fall back down, leaving a number of companies on the verge of bankruptcy. Second, recent reports indicate that most online businesses are making money and the stock shakeup is actually good for E-Commerce. Third, much of the discussion centering on E-Commerce economics relates to traditional business operations. However, many nontraditional businesses are finding a home on the Internet, and are succeeding.

Internet Investments

http://www.ecommercetimes.com/news/articles2000/000725-2.shtml

Until recently, inflated market valuations for Internet companies were so commonplace, it seemed as though the financial world had been turned upside down and inside out. There was no way to determine realistic market values for Internet stocks—no history, no precedents. While revenues were crowned king, hype actually ruled. Anyone who had achieved some measure of success in the technology domain quickly ascended to the upper level and drew investor confidence measured in the millions (US$). So did any company that had a good idea—especially if it entailed adding the term "dot.com" to a company's name.

In retrospect, a number of the E-Commerce ventures that experienced the heady rise and dizzying fall of their stock values had been marked for endangerment—if not extinction—rather than near-term profitability. Following stunning initial public offerings, some dot-coms burned through cash so fast that they were forced to make repeated pilgrimages to the venture capital holy land, looking for new investors or trying to stir up interest in possible mergers. As confidence waned, new rounds of financing were required, causing stock prices to fall. Even the highest flyers were forced into lower earth orbits.

The litany of failures began. A raft of little-known companies faded into oblivion, and some big players—like Peapod, Homegrocer, Boo.com and CDNow—were bought out at bargain prices. The latest conclusions and prognostications are based on the performances of a few emerging bellwethers. Barron's reported in March 2000 that startups and smaller E-Commerce entities were not the only companies that were cash poor. According to the report, sixty Internet companies, including Amazon, were expected to run out of cash within one year. Amazon would be tapped out in 10.08 months, the report claimed. The welcome news for investors who have felt lost at sea over the past couple of years, is that a good old-fashioned analysis of how well a business model is working may once again be a strong indicator of a company's likelihood for success. A number of companies are back on the right track, currently selling shares at realistic prices. The reality is that some of them may not weather the storm—but to anyone who has ever dipped a toe into the stock market's turbulent waters, that should be a given. The reality is also that those who do survive will probably never soar the way they soared before

A recent report states, "To please the Street, online merchants will balance marketing blitzes with a new focus on company fundamentals following their first-quarter earnings announcements." As a result, Forrester contends that 2000 was a year of widespread e-tailer consolidation, as startups huddled together for competitive leverage while brick-and-mortar giants bought the talent, technologies and processes needed to put them in the online arena (**http://www.ecommercetimes.com/news/articles2000/000131-4.shtml**). Convergence may become the critical buzzword, as businesses realize that traditional stores and e-tail Web sites are not necessarily mutually exclusive (**http://www.ecommercetimes.com/news/articles/991230-1.shtml**). The shopper who bought apparel from *gapinc.com* and finds that he or she can return it to The Gap store at the local mall is apt to shop the site again.

Concise, easily accessible product information may be key to closing a sale. According to results of a survey from the Software and Information Industry Association (SIIA), it is not just infrastructure and fulfillment problems that are challenging e-tailers. The survey found that 17 percent of survey respondents needed additional information about a product while shopping online.

Success

http://www.ecommercetimes.com/news/viewpoint2000/ view-000127-1.shtml

One of the great stereotypes about dot-com companies is that they are all bleeding red ink despite raising millions of dollars (US$) in well-publicized Silicon Valley IPOs. However, a survey by Ernst & Young debunks that myth. The research, which was based on 150 telephone interviews with CEOs of Internet companies, found that while leaders like e-tail giant Amazon.com are operating in the red, 69 percent of the companies surveyed are profitable. One example of a profitable E-Commerce company is eBay, Inc., which reported a FY2000 fourth-quarter operating profit as sales more than doubled and an additional 305,000 users were attracted to its site. The San Jose, California-based online auctioneer reported that net income rose to $4.9 million as compared with $3.9 million one year ago. Additionally, sales rose 139 percent to $73.9 million from $30.9 million.

According to the Ernst & Young study, eBay is more typical of dot-com enterprises than Amazon. Two out of three Internet companies surveyed in the study indicated that they are making money, and half of that number claim to have no intention of going public. "Perhaps surprisingly, 69 percent of online businesses we surveyed are in fact profitable," Ernst & Young partner Roger Savell told the Bloomberg Forum. "Most are small and highly-focused," he added.

In all the news reports, about struggling and failing e-tailers, the same message is often buried somewhere toward the bottom of the page, if not hidden between the lines (**http://www.ecommercetimes.com/news/articles2000/000706-2.shtml**). The message implies that the loss of the weak members of the E-Commerce community—while devastating for them—is a good thing for the industry as a whole.

Through consolidation, E-Commerce is strengthening its core and building credibility. The venture capital and investment funding that once flowed so liberally to so many spindly little branches is being re-routed to feed the roots and the trunk of the E-Commerce tree.

Internet Gambling

http://www.ecommercetimes.com/news/articles2000/000817-2.shtml

Besides the traditional areas of commerce, the Internet has also entered into other non-traditional areas of commerce, such as gambling. The Internet hosts over 700 online gaming sites, generating billions of dollars (US$) in revenue. Internet gambling expanded into a $1.1 billion industry in 1999, a sum that is expected to increase to $3 billion by 2002, according to gambling industry consulting firm the River City Group.

While online gaming is worth billions of dollars in cyberspace, it's benefits are not enjoyed by real-world cities and communities. Critics argue that online gaming cannot help construct a tourist industry or generate economic growth in a city or Native American reservation. Ultimately, the largest issues facing the online gaming industry are the legal uncertainties. The report, "World Online Gambling Markets," examines the industry for its growth and its vulnerabilities to government regulation and competitive changes. (**http://www.ecommercetimes.com/news/articles/991012-2.shtml**)

Internet gambling generated $834.5 million (US$) in 1998, an increase of more than 100 percent over 1997 revenues. Moreover, analysts expect online gambling software and operations to continue to grow sharply over the next five years.

Despite the high profile, the researchers report that gambling operators and software developers see little legal threat because the laws prohibiting online gambling are effectively unenforceable. Therefore, they say, gambling operators are marching forward in the face of the legal uncertainties and into the arms of exploding markets in Europe and Asia.

The report contends that the legal questions and enforcement uncertainties continue in the online gambling world because there is no regulatory body to bring it out of the shadows. However, it continues, any intervention by the U.S. government would come with a whole other set of repercussions. "If the U.S. government opts to regulate Internet gambling," said the Frost & Sullivan's report author, "it will open the floodgates to the Harrah's and Caesar's of the world to establish online operations and essentially drive the lesser-known operations out of the market."

QUESTIONS

1. What does the report, "World Online Gambling Markets," suggest that some operators need to deliver to survive competition from the major offline operators?
(http://www.ecommercetimes.com/news/articles/991012-2.shtml)

2. How have the initial pricing for shares for an initial offering been determined for internet stocks?
(http://www.ecommercetimes.com/news/articles/991012-2.shtml)

3. What are the topics of most customer complaints and what must an e-tailer do to solve these problems?
(http://www.ecommercetimes.com/news/articles/991230-1.shtml)

CHAPTER 5:
CONSUMER MOTIVATION FOR
E-COMMERCE USE

This chapter provides a general overview of consumer usage of the Internet to conduct transactions, and discusses why, and why not, consumers buy online.

E-Commerce Today

http://cism.bus.utexas.edu/

According to the University of Texas Center for Research in Electric Commerce semiannual study investigating more than 3,000 businesses, the Internet economy directly supported nearly 2.5 million jobs in 1999—an increase of 650,000 over 1998's figure. That means more people now toil in the new economy than do within the federal government (excluding postal workers). The authors define Net companies as those that "leverage the Internet for business." They include not only outfits such as Amazon.com, which conduct business solely on the Web, but also the Internet-related revenues of companies such as Toys "R" Us, which sell both online and off.

It's not just a question of traffic as measured by "head-count". Net-related revenues, the report finds, jumped 62 percent in 2000—fifteen times the rate for the U.S. economy as a whole—to $524 billion. "The data confirm that there is a new economy, and that it is growing very rapidly," says Deutsche Bank Alex Brown chief global investment strategist Ed Yardeni. Though the report was commissioned by Cisco Systems, Yardeni and others say its findings shouldn't be discounted—this isn't the new-economy equivalent of the tobacco industry's "neutral" studies on the health effects of cigarettes. "The industry needed a benchmark," says Wes Basel, senior economist at Regional Financial Associates in West Chester, Pa. "This is it."

The authors, University of Texas Business School professors Andrew Whinston and Anitesh Barua, break the Internet economy into four layers: infrastructure (companies such as Cisco and Lucent), applications (Adobe, Oracle), intermediary (Yahoo.com, e*trade.com), and commerce (Amazon.com). Whinston and Barua found that the most dramatic revenue-per-employee spikes occurred in the E-Commerce (37 percent) and intermediary (30 percent) layers. The four-layer breakdown has led some critics to accuse the authors of double- counting. "You don't want to count the wheat that was grown, then the miller's flour, and then the bread itself," says Steven Landefeld, director of the Federal Bureau of Economic Analysis. "If you count each one of those sales, you will come up with bread that costs $3 when it actually costs only $1.50." Landefeld charges that the report overstates the Internet industry's size nearly twofold.

The authors vehemently deny that they're overstating the size of the Net economy. The report seeks to capture something different from GDP, they argue. "We are looking at revenue growth, and GDP is a notion of value added," says Whinston. "We are just looking at things differently." As a result, the report does break out the sales (to continue the metaphor) of wheat, flour, and bread in the figures for each layer of the Net economy—but then it subtracts the overlap in calculating the figures that combine the various layers.

Michael Cox, chief economist of the Dallas Federal Reserve, dismisses doubts about the methodology. "[Questions] usually come from people who have yesterday's understanding, which is by sector," he says. "The Internet is not a sector. It's a way of doing business." E-Commerce companies—widely maligned by stock mavens and media commentators—saw revenues skyrocket in 1999, surging 72 percent, to $171.5 billion, according to the report, making it the fastest-growing of the layers and the second-largest behind infrastructure itself ($198 billion).

The research has left Whinston bullish on the prospects of the Net economy. "More and more companies are finding ways to exploit layers one [infrastructure] and two [applications]," he says, adding, "1999 was the year the seesaw tipped and people stopped asking why the highway was built."

Why People Buy Online

http://www.wharton.upenn.edu/news/news_rel/wvtm.html

The results of the Wharton Virtual Test Market indicate that the rate of growth of online spending per person is declining even though total online retail spending is increasing. In addition, findings from the study published in the *Journal of Interactive Marketing* revealed a significant dropout rate of online shoppers. Fifteen percent of the consumers who bought online in 1997 did not buy online in 1998. No matter how well electronic retailers have done, there are some fundamental factors that appear to be eroding the growth of spending and the growth of the market," said Jerry Lohse, research director of the Wharton Forum on Electronic Commerce, which sponsors the Wharton Virtual Test Market. "Only 50% of the dropouts from 1998 returned to make a purchase in

1999. Further, new buyers are not arriving as quickly to take their place. The implication is that online shopping is just another way of shopping."

People buy online for convenience. For example, one predictor of whether someone will buy online is travel time to the nearest music store. The farther away someone is from a music store, the more likely they will buy online. As reported by Lohse, Steve Bellman and Eric Johnson in the December 1999 issue of the *Communications of the ACM,* lack of time and a "wired lifestyle," not demographics, are important predictors of online buying behavior. In addition, increased experience with using the Internet, higher numbers of hours online at home, use of the web for financial services and a significant reliance on email all increased the likelihood of spending online.

The Wharton Virtual Test Market has tracked more than 23,000 panelists since 1997, including preliminary results from 791 participants who have been on the panel for all three years. These same-sample studies have shown a slowing in spending by the same individual over time. Other studies are just beginning to note the dropout phenomenon and the slower growth of consumers coming online. *Cyber Dialogue* reported that 27 million U.S. adults gave up using the Internet this year.

What are the implications of this apparent slowing of growth? Many forecasts for E-Commerce spending and market growth assume linear increases in per person online spending. The current Wharton results indicate that those forecasts may need to be revised downward. Based on the latest Virtual Test Market survey, Wharton research estimate current levels of consumer online spending at about $29.2 billion and project that that Internet retail sales will climb to $133 billion by January 2004.

Slower growth would have tremendous implications for the growth of Business-to-Consumer markets and the future of "dot com" firms that are projecting the escalating use of the Internet. This may be time for a reality check," said Lohse. He noted that the study, although it is one of the most comprehensive longitudinal surveys of E-Commerce, still is based on only three years of data. "There is much more to learn about the market—particularly as more products become available for consumers to buy online."

Harry Hoyle of Dataquest says three things drive E-Commerce: convenience, cost, and context. (**http://www.zdnet.com/anchordesk/stories/story/0,10738,2563430,00.html**) Nearly three-quarters of shoppers interviewed by Dataquest cited convenience as the reason they shop online. The Internet has allowed vendors from all parts of the world to inexpensively showcase their goods, in a central marketplace. If your product or service is something that is sold exclusively through the Internet, or it's relatively hard to find otherwise, mention this fact on your Web site. It could create an even greater demand for what you're offering. Referring to cost, some 38 percent of online shoppers say they bought on the Web because it was less expensive. As to context, people use the Internet for different activities: work, recreation, research, and entertainment.

Retailers need to be able to present consumers with the opportunity to buy online at the right time, in the right place. Some sites make it incredibly difficult to order online. There are many options that you can add or do to your site, such as: (1) maintain a link to your ordering information on every, single page of your site; (2) if you have more than five products, make sure you have a shopping cart on your site; (3) don't expect prospects to write down names of products and buying codes; and (4) offer prospects the opportunity to order by secure server, telephone, fax and snail-mail. Some allow wire transfers, and payment by Western Union.

Reasons Consumers Do Not Buy Online

http://www.wharton.upenn.edu/news/news_rel/wvtm.html

What factors contribute to the decline in online spending growth? Concerns about privacy and trust were among the most important factors that distinguished buyers from non-buyers online, according to the Wharton study. "People are primarily dropping out for privacy or security issues,—or because they've had a bad shopping experience online and want to deal with a real person. For example, try exchanging an airline ticket online," Lohse said. Concern about "monitoring by third parties" was the highest predictor for not purchasing online and an unwillingness to "trust the business with private data" was also very significant.

How do people react to E-Commerce as a new experience? Ninety-seven percent of surfers indicate they are uncomfortable submitting credit card data online. And with the recent information about hacking, that suspicion is probably going to remain for a while, even though efforts are under way to help ameliorate the situation (**http://www.senate.gov/~bennett/breakfast_session.html**). The second largest reason (54 percent) why people do not buy online is customer service problems, such as: 18 percent complain they couldn't talk to a sales representative; 16 percent stated that they couldn't get enough product information on the web to make an intelligent decision; 11 percent worried the process took too long; and 10 percent stressed the web site was too hard to navigate and just went some place else. Finally, 53 percent want to see the product before the purchase, while 11 percent said they had to download special software, and they lacked skills necessary to accomplish the task.

QUESTIONS

1. What are a few of the things you can do to your website to make it easier for consumers?
(http://www.wharton.upenn.edu/news/news_rel/wvtm.html)

2. What are the Internet's Four Layers , as described by the University of Texas Business School professors Andrew Whinston and Anitesh Barua ?
(http://www.wharton.upenn.edu/news/news_rel/wvtm.html)

3. Briefly describe the Wharton Virtual Test Model and its findings.
(http://www.wharton.upenn.edu/news/news_rel/wvtm.html)

CHAPTER 6:
SECURITY FOR CONSUMERS

According to a number of studies, a major concern for Internet users is security. Consumers are concerned with security during transactions, as well as, protecting their privacy online. By all indications, E-Commerce will continue to grow. However, businesses online must demonstrate that they are protecting consumer privacy and all transactions taking place in the virtual environment. Consumers will eventually move their business to reputable sites that vigorously support consumers' security and privacy.

Transaction Integrity and Security

http://builder.cnet.com/Business/Ecommerce20/ss03.html/

As the number of transactions online increases, pressure regarding Internet security increases. Ironically, Internet businesses and experts argue that Internet transactions are less dangerous than those completed in the physical world. One of the main reasons for this is a great deal of credit card fraud is caused by retail employees that handle the cards. E-Commerce transactions make this impossible by encrypting the numbers on company servers. Another reason that experts argue E-Commerce is safer is that there is no "brick-and-mortar" store that can be robbed, burned, or ransacked.

E-Commerce businesses ensure consumers that E-Commerce transactions, if done properly, are safer. Many consumers, including those that complete transactions online on a regular basis, do not yet believe that E-Commerce transactions are more secure than transactions completed in the physical world.

Protecting Consumers

www.ecommercetimes.com/news/articles2000/000425-1a.shtml

Secure Sockets Layer (SSL) is a protocol that creates a secure connection to a server protecting information as it travels over the Internet. This has been available to Internet users since the 2.0 versions of Netscape Navigator and Microsoft Internet Explorer were released. One can tell that a website is secured by SSL when the URL begins with *https* instead of *http*. The "s" stands for "secure."

An additional security application, Secure Electronic Transactions (SET), is also being promoted by credit card companies and browser makers as the ultimate security for Internet transactions. SET encodes credit card numbers entered during a transaction into a business server so that only banks and credit card companies can read the numbers. Unless a hacker is able to decipher the encryption during the transaction, which is virtually impossible, the transaction is safe. Although no system can yet guarantee 100 percent security for a credit card, if one takes precautions they are safer than shopping in the local mall.

Privacy, by far, is the most important issue to online purchasers today. Privacy advocates believe that if something is not done to calm consumers fears, then confidence in E-Commerce will decrease, and the Federal Trade Commission will attempt to aggressively regulate the industry. Others feel that regulation is not necessary and that consumers must exercise self-control. They believe that as consumers become educated, they will not use those sites that act unethically. Both sides feel that they are correct; however, the problem still exists.

There has been a great deal of controversy recently regarding privacy and the collecting and sharing of personal data. One of the best known examples recently occurred when Internet advertising company DoubleClick purchased Abacus Direct Corp. Double Click owned a technology called DART that allowed it to track the behavior of browsers on the Internet in order to better target advertising. At the time it did not link this to the identities of users. However, after the purchase of Abacus, it began linking the anonymous information to Abacus's database of names, addresses and telephone numbers. Even though DoubleClick stated that it only linked those users who have given it permission the FTC, the states of New York and Michigan began to investigate. DoubleClick was also investigated for placing cookies onto users' computers to track the sites they visited. DoubleClick has since attempted to control negative publicity by announcing that it would not continue to link personally identifiable information to any anonymous user and has hired consumer advocates to lead it privacy efforts. According to some in the industry, DoubleClick's problem was not that it invaded users' privacy, but that it changed its privacy policy and did not let anyone know. Many companies get in trouble because they give consumers the opportunity to opt out, but do not necessarily give them the option to opt in.

In many cases, consumers automatically give their permission for organizations to gather information if they do not opt out. It is irrelevant whether or not they opted in. When consumers find this out they are not happy. Some experts believe the opt-in method that gives consumers the opportunity to give permission with respect to each item of personal data is the most ethical way to protect consumers' privacy.

Critics of the opt-in method state that it is an inconvenience to consumers and tends to make them reject a particular site. They prefer the opt-out method, which allows consumers to withhold permission to collect personal data. Others argue that the opt-out method requires that consumer opt-out, if they do not want personal data collected. Either way, online organizations must address the privacy issue

Determining Reputable Sites

http://www.safeshopping.org/seller/index.html

With all of the security and privacy issues on the Internet, how can a consumer determine which sites are reputable and which sites should be avoided? With the cost of putting a website on the Internet relatively low, anyone can publish their opinions or set up an online store to sell just about anything. There are, however, precautions that consumers can take to help them determine reputable websites.

First, most people are more comfortable dealing with companies and organizations they know. The same is true online. If you are not familiar with the name and reputation of the company, especially if you have received an unsolicited e-mail, find out as much as you can before you purchase. This goes for consumer purchases, as well as business purchases. The Better Business Bureau is an excellent source of information about companies online. Keep in mind however, that websites are an excellent way for criminals to be anonymous. Likewise, new websites are started all the time and it is impossible for the Better Business Bureau to track them all. Tips for determining reputable sites include:

Avoid spam. Although many e-mails ask you to reply if you would like your name removed from a list, some experts advise against responding. This because your e-mail may be sold to other sites. It is best to contact your Internet Service Provider. Also, most companies that use spam are less than reputable.

Know the seller by more than a website. Will the seller be there tomorrow? If you have problems, do you have a phone number or address (not Post Office Box) to contact someone for assistance.

Are you buying from someone outside the United States? If so, beware that you may not have the same legal rights as you would if the seller were located in the United States.

Does the seller have experience selling the item? The law gives you more protection if you buy an item from a seller who regularly sells the particular item.

Is the company an authorized seller? You will typically get a warranty if you purchase from an authorized seller. If you are unsure, check with the manufacturer before purchasing.

Be leery of shopping for the lowest price. Be aware that some sellers have taken technological steps to block these "agents" from gathering pricing data. In addition, "agent" sites might not take shipping costs or return/refund policies into account when comparing the prices.

Is the seller still selling? You may want to telephone or send an e-mail to determine if the seller is still in operation, particularly, if the site looks old or outdated.

By following these steps, many consumers will save themselves a lot of headaches.

QUESTIONS

1. Why do many experts believe that transactions are safer when completed on the Internet verses in the physical world at a retail store? (**http://builder.cnet.com/Business/Ecommerce20/ss03.html/**)

2. List at least 5 things that a consumer can do to determine if an online business is reputable. (**www.safeshopping.org/seller/index.html**)

3. What are the arguments for and against "opt-in" and "opt-out" solutions? (**www.ecommercetimes.com/news/articles2000/000425-1a.shtml**) Hint (Go to continue at bottom of website to go to page 2)

CHAPTER 7:
SECURITY SYSTEMS for
E-COMMERCE

Connecting to the Internet creates potential opportunities for a company, as well as numerous risks. Companies address these issues by focusing on hardware and software needed to keep hackers and viruses from invading their websites and Internet networks. Although hardware and software considerations represent only one layer of security, key strategic tactics include: (1) implementing solid security measures; and (2) establishing policies and procedures that require users and network administrators to take precautions with their passwords, website activity, and IT support. Ironically, 80 percent of all security threats are generated from within a corporation by disgruntled employees. This happens when unauthorized software is placed on a network, or websites are visited that obtain internal information. The most common threat involves non-authorized employee passwords gaining access to the network system (**http://www.wws.prince-ton.edu/cgi-bin/byteserv.prl/~ota/disk1/1995/9513/951303.PDF**).

Network Threats

http://www.ecommercetimes.com/news/articles/990726-1.shtml
http://www.ecommercetimes.com/news/articles/2000/000210-4.shtml

Hackers continue to invent new techniques for accessing internal net-works and personal computers. The web site, **http://www.alt2600.com**, provides information on the latest locations that have been attacked by hackers. This site also highlights the techniques and tools the hackers have used to gain access. The website is supported by the U.S. government to help prevent communication problems caused by hacker activity.

Port Entrance

http://207.96.11.93/Encryption/Default.htm

An easy entrance for any hacker is an open port. Interestingly, all web-site open portals can be obtained by using a free piece of software, Portscan 1.2, which is available on the Internet. This program was developed by a security firm to check the safety of its customers websites; however the program fell into the wrong hands and now is used to find loopholes in the security setup of a website. This program also finds FTP and Internet services on any assigned port link that might open up the website. Aditionally, programs such as IP-Prober allow a user to scan open ports and determine when the website is schedule for maintenance, which ensures it will be open and access can be obtained. **(http://www.infowar.com)**

Oracle admitted to hiring a detective firm using this style of website espionage. They were attempting to determine why certain groups were being sympathetic to Microsoft during their recent antitrust battle with the US Government. Ironically, as this story broke several others were made public; each issue involved disgruntled employee, who had access to their networks and opened an electronic "trapdoor" for hackers to gain access to the company's and their customer's private information. Price lists, research and development plans, strategic plans, customer's buying list, can all be obtained during some of these hacking sessions. Unfortunately, once these hackers gain access the trapdoors remain open forever, unless the hacker does harm like planting a virus bomb. This is according to Mike Ackerman, a retired CIA operative, who indicated this is the most common type of hacking offense. Without an insider's assistance, most low budget hackers could not gain access to large organizations systems network (**http://www.infowar.com**).

To offset this problem, many firms hire service agents, such as DefCon, who for a fee, practice hacking into the company's server so that alternative security measurements can be put in place to prevent this from happening by a real hacking team. Often these companies are called "the black hat community", because most of the really successful firms consist of former hackers, who have been prosecuted by law. Many large corporations do not believe in hiring these services from the "black hat community", because they feel they are funding the hacking problem. Typically the companies who complain the most about hackers are the companies who have the most activity from hackers attempting to break into their websites (**http://www.globetechnology.com/archieves/gam/news/20000822 /routs.html**).

Password Cracking

http://www.ecommercetimes.com/news/articles2000/0210-4.shtml

The oldest method hackers employ to gain access to networks is simply cracking the access passwords. Although initially started as a game, this has become a competitive espionage tool to extract information on competitors. Tools are available on the Internet that can generate series of combinations of letters and numbers to crack any password code. Many network providers use a tool called Crack, that can be downloaded free from **http://www.cert.org**. The site allows users to check passwords and determine the level of difficulty it would take to crack. The more alphanumeric combinations a password has, the more secure the password. The largest offense of password decoding happened in March 2000, when hackers broke into E*Trade's website and created loop bombs in many customer's accounts. Fortunately, no one's funds were touched, but this team of pranksters caused the online broker to shut down for a day and reduced the speed Internet transactions within the websites, linked to E*Trade's website. A loop bomb has a customer's account number to start opening sites within the website. This process goes on until the website crashes due to excess activity. Typically this process takes 10-25 minutes, once the website has been penetrated.

Virus Intrusion

http://www.ecommercetimes.com/news/articles/2000/000209-3.shtml

Virus exposure has dramatically increased as the use of e-mail has become more and more predominant among employees, customers and suppliers. Depending on the type of virus encoding, work files, execution files, or even work macro files may be attacked. A virus attack can be quite disrupting to the server, especially if execution files are targeted for disruptuion. This happened in February, 2000, when hackers made planned attacks on some of the Internet's largest web companies: Yahoo!, Amazon.com, and eBay. These sites were penetrated, a virus was planted, leaving users or potential buyers with "denial-of-service" messages. "It is like a revolving door spinning. A few people could get in and shop, but the majority of our traffic was blocked by this attack," said Buy.com's CEO Gregory Hawkins, after the web retailer was shut down for 1.5 days due to hacking activity.

The latest series of attacks have drawn additional attention from the FBI to saboteur's activity. It is believed that instead of traditional hacker activities, these latest series of viral attacks could be targeted against US companies by hostile foreign nations, in attempt to harm the US economy. The US government has developed a task force to investigate these recent claims.

Even with encrypted technology, online retailers have grave concern for their data safety. Once a hacker has gained access to a website's core information such as customer credit cards, checking accounts, or even electronic funds transfers numbers, the hacker has broken a confidence level that may never restored between the buyer and seller.

Virus and Hacker's Tools

http://www.ecommercetimes.com/news/articles2000/00209-3.shtml

Technology used by hackers has focused on the "ping" command. This command can be used to exploit the computer system, as most systems use this sound to indicate a new message has arrived on your Internet service provider. The program is free, on the Internet, to whoever wants to download it. This type of virus attack begins with a small message, but it multiples logarithmically in size. Known as a "looping technique" it can crash a network server within minutes. As it pertains to E-Commerce websites, this type of hacking technique can actually prevent the firm from selling products or services on-line. For example, the majority of E-Commerce hacking activity has impacted the pornography industry. Tools such as Sscan, Telnet, and other FTP technology allow the hackers to open the pornographic websites and allow anyone to have free access instead of paying for the services provided to the visitors of the websites.

A new industry has been developed to combat hacking, known as the "white hat community", which prevents hackers from gaining access to websites. This is done without attempting to break into the website as a means of protecting it like the "black hat community". The companies in the "white hat community" use technology to make the website data storage facilities more secure. Companies like nCiper.com have developed two independent systems to prevent hackers from penetrating websites and obtaining access to valuable private information.

First Solution is a software system that makes it difficult for hackers to obtain information, by layering the website so that information is found within a three-dimensional network, thus making simple data extraction not possible. Common data warehouse systems use single spreadsheet or multiple two dimensional spreadsheets to store data. By use of a three dimensional spreadsheet the data extraction technique is much more complicated. Also nCiper.com has installed alarm systems within the three dimensional network to alert the organization if someone has been in the data recently.

The second solution is a non-internal website database for sensitive data. This data storage facility is on a closed internal network that must go through a series of passages before the information is available. The benefit of this type of system is that it protects the data. The downside is the system is extremely slow, due to the large number of passages the network has to flow to save the integrity of the data.

Finally, in early January 2000, a bill that would allow the sale of encrypted technology to other countries was signed into law by the US government. Now any encryption commodity, software, or hardware server, can be sold outside the US by a US company. The technology export policy also limits the sales of this type of technology to foreign governments. Many other strong software-developing nations have adopted similar rules against selling encryption technology to other foreign nations. However the negative side of this law is that as the World Wide Web is global in nature, Internet users will have access to information that may not be protected. Also due to access limitation for this technology, trade to foreign countries may be affected.

Firewall Security

http://www.ntresearch.com/firewall.htm

A firewall consists of a server and two network interface cards. The external network card communicates with the Internet or extranet and the internal network card communicates between the Internet or internal network. Typically a firewall is placed between the internal servers and the external servers, and depending upon the design, provides protection against external users accessing the internal network. Firewalls provide a method of filtering information that is transmitted over the network. A proxy server is another mechanism to separate network net service from the Internet. Proxy servers operate similar to firewalls, but mediates between the client's requests within the company, such as Http requests from a browser, and servers outside the firewall. Proxy servers mask the return address, providing an additional layer of secure anonymity for users and denying potential targets. It is within these proxy servers that most virus software package are contained.

Since the "Love Bug" virus in early 2000, most websites and servers have updated their technology to include a security firewall program that denies all outsiders access to port 80, resulting in no one from outside the organization accessing the HTTP server. Thus, the reason recent hacking activity has been traced to internal disgruntled employees (http://www.sterling.com/firewall.html).

Encryption

http://204.193.246.62/public.nsf/docs/60D6B47456BB389F8525686 40078B6C0#a

Encryption is a term used to describe secret coding of data. Encryption techniques involve the transformation of data to a scrambled form, which cannot be read or interpreted without the appropriate knowledge or translation key. Thus encryption and decryption require the use of common information. Latest versions of encryption technology use algorithms to scramble and unscramble data from a three dimensional network of data. This technology complicates potential hackers by a logarithmic factor of extracting information from encrypted codes.

There are several types of encryption codes: Symmetric Key Encryption features a single key to encrypt and decrypt information. As with all encrypted codes, this requires parties have the same symmetric key code. An Asymmetric Key Encryption requires two complementary keys to encrypt and decrypt information: a private key and a public key. The public key, freely distributed, is only used for encryption and is not able to decrypt any encrypted documents or files. Only the complementary private key can decrypt the information.

In addition to the above, the website Pretty Good Privacy (http://www.pgp.com) offers a free software program, which can be downloaded from the Internet. The software is acceptable for private use, but is insufficient for commercial use, thus a private version should be purchased for your company's needs. A private program will automatically create public/private keys and key rings. Distribution of the keys or decoders can be provided on an as-needed basis. Encryption and decryption algorithms are the backbone for most encryption technology. Rivest, Shamir and Adleman (RSA) algorithms are the most popular formulas which start by generating a very large prime number for a public key code, then from this backbone large prime numbers create a custom decoder sequence.

QUESTIONS

1. Explain how the software industry removes themselves from liability concerning security. Who is legally responsible for security Snafus? (**http://www.ecommercetimes.com/news/viewpoint2000/view-000831-1.shtml**)

2. Truste, an organization that monitors Internet privacy issues, was recently caught using technology that violates its own privacy policy through the use of a third-party software program, which obtains private information from website visitors. Discuss the rationale Truste and others justify the use of this type of privacy violation. (**http://www.ecommerce-times.com/news/articles2000/000825-3.shtml**)

3. Can network systems be assesses by unauthorized users? If yes, please explain what areas these unauthorized users have access to; if no, please explain how these prevention mechanisms work (**http://www.ecommercetimes.com/news/articles/990726-1.shtml**)

CHAPTER 8:
DISTRIBUTION

Businesses and entrepreneurs view E-Commerce as the new growth sector of the economy. Manufacturers that have always sold directly to retailers are now attempting to sell to consumers online. What many businesses and entrepreneurs fail to take into consideration is, how the products and services offered online will be distributed. How will the orders be filled? How will products be shipped? Overall, how does the product finally reach the consumer? Many organizations are finding that these questions are the hardest part about selling online. At the same time these manufacturers see the future and do not want to be left behind, thus seek ways to best distribute products to the consumer.

Order Fulfillment

http://ecommerce.internet.com/solutions/e-consultant/article/0,1467,9571_125441,00.html

Those firms new to E-Commerce retailing are finding that getting products to the customer is one of the difficult aspects of selling on the Internet. They design the website, the shopping cart, and the payment system. The customers come, but no one determined the best way to get the products to the consumers.

E-Commerce retailers must learn that the Internet is just another channel for business to be conducted and many of the basic business rules apply, including order fulfillment. As with any mail order business (that is what E-Commerce is), getting products to customers can be costly, in more ways than just money. If an E-Commerce retailer cannot get products to consumers in a timely manner, then the consumers will shop elsewhere. Many businesses use order fulfillment services to ease the burden on resources, however there are some important things of which to be aware.

The primary purpose of using a fulfillment service is to get products to the consumers consistently, while keeping control of inventory and delivery confirmations. It allows E-Commerce retailers to focus on what they are good at: marketing, product development, and sales. It also allows the fulfillment center to provide the service in which it specializes: order fulfillment.

Different types of fulfillment services exist, offering a variety of options. An E-Commerce retailer needs to evaluate which type serves its needs. Services can range from simple distribution to order process, customer service, quality control, and even billing. Fill-It Inc. offers a complete E-Commerce solution providing E-Commerce retailers a link to their E-Commerce engine. There, customers use a shopping cart to select goods from the retailer's site and place orders. Fill-It Inc. processes the payment, sends out an invoice and fills the order.

It is obvious that fulfillment services offer solutions, but E-Commerce retailers must determine their fulfillment needs first before choosing a type of fulfillment service. Many experts suggest working backward by determining the logistics. How fast must the product be delivered? How fast can inventory be replenished? What are the costs and how much can the retailer afford charge the customer for shipping and handling. This must be done before the website is developed. A temptation exists for people to adopt a "get rich quick" mentality concerning potential opportunities on the Internet, and thus do not logically think through the distribution system, or for that matter, the entire business plan.

Just as E-Commerce retailers must find the fulfillment center that works best for them, fulfillment centers must be selective about obtaining clients. Large businesses with a steady flow of products are the favorite choice among fulfillment services. Fulfillment services also prefer Business-to-Business customers over consumer sites. Small items, such as CD's and videos, are preferred by fulfillment services because they can use a variety of shipping packaging and are usually sold in high volume. Fulfillment centers can afford to be selective, due the growth in Internet transactions over the last few years.

Shipping

www.ecommercetimes.com/small_business/strategy/grip.shtml

E-Commerce retailers may spend a great deal of time and money developing an effective website, but sometimes forget the most important elements of retailing. Consumers take all costs into consideration, whether buying online or in a store. It is not an uncommon experience for online shoppers to find a product they want to purchase, put it in their shopping cart and prepare to pay, then discover that the cost of shipping is more than the cost of the product itself. The shopping cart is emptied and the transaction abruptly ends. Unfortunately, E-Commerce retailers cannot sell to consumers if their shipping model does not make sense.

In many cases online, a "catalog shipping model" is used where the shipping and handling fees are tied as a percentage of the price of the product being shipping. Experts argue that this makes no sense, because the consumer is penalized for spending more money at an online store. The more they spend, the more they must pay in shipping costs. They argue that the model should be reversed. The consumer should be rewarded for spending more money on a website.

Consumers are becoming increasingly educated as they make more purchases online. E-Commerce retailers that have the power to negotiate a flat rate for each item shipped possess a competitive advantage. However, considering that many E-Commerce businesses are still relatively small, that is not always the case.

E-Commerce retailers may elect to offer free shipping. This has some advantages and disadvantages. Obviously, it is an attractive incentive to consumers and may motivate them to purchase from that site. On the other hand, someone must pay the shipping bill and if the consumer does not, then the E-Commerce retailer does. This cost is either absorbed by the business in lower profits or passed on to the consumer in the form of higher prices. Experts argue that once a business offers free shipping, it is very hard to charge for shipping in future transactions. Educated consumers do not want to pay for shipping if they have not had to in times past.

One solution to the shipping problem may be simply calculating the actual cost to ship a product and charging the consumer this actual price. Many software packages are available that will calculate the cost of getting a product from one point to the other with just the addresses, weight and dimensions. Consumers seem more willing to pay an actual shipping cost instead of a percentage and retailers do not lose money as they do with free shipping.

Channel Management

www.ecommercetimes.com/news/articles2000/000107-5.shtml

A number of manufacturers are moving into the arena of selling direct to consumers online. This, however, is causing resentment from the distribution channels that made them a success in the "bricks and mortar" world. As manufacturers increase selling efforts online, it will be interesting to see whether or not they are able to bypass their typical distribution channels and sell directly to the consumer. If they are successful, it will raise the issue of why distributors are even needed in the first place. This is, of course, something distributors do not want to hear, thus creating "channel conflict."

Channel conflict is the situation that arises as manufacturers, wholesalers, distributors, retailers, and E-Commerce retailers all attempts to come up with the best strategy to participate in the E-Commerce arena. They are attempting to do this without angering their "bricks and mortar" sales agents and partners.

This is a serious situation for numerous organizations. E-Commerce retailers have stated that they may quit dealing with certain manufacturers if these manufacturers continue to sell directly to consumers online. Some E-Commerce retailers do have this kind of leverage, but many do sell enough to make this a viable threat. In the future however, that may change.

Manufacturers, looking for quick profits, may find that E-Commerce is harder than originally estimated. There is a high cost to running a first rate E-Commerce site. Manufacturers are typically experienced in making huge warehouse deliveries, as compared to the individual consumer deliveries that E-Commerce retailers often make. These problems, topped with the fact that retailers and distributors are not happy competing against the manufacturer, may be enough to keep many out of the market. Still, there are success stories of manufacturers selling online. Dell Computers has had great success online, but it has always sold directly to consumers. Many of the issues that other manufacturers face have been resolved years ago by Dell.

Manufacturers are driven by the thoughts of increased profits that can come from selling directly to consumers and bypassing the distributors, resellers, and retailers. Imagine the profits that can be achieved if a manufacturer is able to successfully sell directly to a consumer and bypass two or three tiers of distribution, such as a manufacturer that sells to a distributor that in turn sells to a retailer.

If manufacturers hope to succeed online, they must strike a balance between E-Commerce direct sales and traditional distribution. There is a way to sell directly to consumers without offending members of the distribution channel. Some manufacturers offer a product line that is only sold on the Internet. Others sell products online under a different name brand. Both of these options often pacify distributors and retailers because they do not feel that they are in direct competition with their suppliers. Still, manufacturers should move slowly as they test the potential of the Internet. The appropriate infrastructure and knowledge are critical to selling online.

QUESTIONS

1. Why is free shipping NOT the best alternative? (**www.ecommerce-times.com/small_business/strategy/grip.shtml**)

2. What two options are recommended if a manufacture wants to sell products online, but at the same time does not want to anger channel partners?
(www.ecommercetimes.com/news/articles2000/000107-5.shtml)

3. What are the six points that are important when choosing a fulfill-ment center? (http://ecommerce.internet.com/solutions/e-consult-ant/article/0,1467,9571_125441,00.html) *Hint: Go to page three of the article.*

CHAPTER 9:
PROMOTION AND MARKETING STRATEGY

E-Commerce is changing the way that many organizations think about promotion and marketing strategy. The Internet is a very powerful marketing tool that can gather a great deal of personal and informative information about consumers. The problem is not gathering the data on consumers, but sorting through the information and using it ethically. If marketers are able to do this, they can then use the information gathered to manage the relationship with customers. Since consumers may not be face-to-face with the seller in a store, it is important that the online marketers use gathered information to develop relationships with their customers. In other words, give them reasons to purchase and continue purchasing. Even with information at their fingertips and the ability to manage customer relationships, marketing is still marketing and the marketing mix is still critical to the success of any organization.

Identifying Customers and Markets

http://interactive.wsj.com/public/current/articles/SB91273067186227
1500.htm

E-Commerce businesses have a distinct advantage over their "bricks and mortar" competitors. They have the ability to gather a great deal a person data about their clients that can aid in developing targeted marketing and selling strategies. A customer's actions in an online store are a two-way electronic link that allows the seller to gather a great deal of information about a customer.

Not only do most online customers supply their names and addresses, but a site can also determine the purchasing history and what the customer looked at, but decided not to buy, i.e. the window shopping. No bricks and mortar store can determine that and the Internet seems like Nirvana to marketers and retailers.

While the technology is available to determine all of the information noted above, most sites are not deploying maximum efficiency. Internet users and advocacy groups have very real concerns about privacy and the use of personal information. Another issue that online retailers face is when to use the data they gather. Is marketing specific products to customers an invasion of privacy, or a service? Also, most Internet sites are busy working out the bugs, setting up inventory management and payment systems and do not have time to analyze the wealth of data their sites generate. E-Commerce is relatively new though and it is only a matter of time before E-Commerce retailers become much more savvy about gathering and analyzing customer data.

Two types of information about customers are available on the Internet. First is the information that customers consciously reveal about themselves. This is the information required for a credit card transaction. It may also include the information that customers fill out on a customer profile form. which may include age, income, and occupation. On the other hand, consumers also reveal a great deal about themselves that they do not realize. For instance, when a consumer first visits a site, the web browser, operating system, country of origin, and Internet Service Provider are logged. The site can also determine how the consumer found the site, if they were forwarded by a hyperlink. As discussed above, the buying patterns of consumers are also easy to track online.

One controversial E-Commerce marketing tactic is the use of cookies. This is a text file, placed by the website on a user's computer, that identifies the consumer when a particular website is visited. Cookies provide marketing with the ability to follow a consumer through the site, determining how long they stay in certain areas and what they purchase. Privacy advocates argue that most consumers do not know they are being followed so closely and fear that the data could be used inappropriately by organizations.

A wealth of information is available on the Internet regarding consumers. The biggest problem is how to decipher what it means. Analysis software and services exist to sort through the data. As valuable and useful as consumer information is to marketers, a tradeoff becomes apparent. Consumers will continue to purchase on the Web in record numbers as long as they feel safe, but if a site abuses a consumer's trust, that consumer will most likely exit the site and never return.

Customer Relationship Management

www.ecommercetimes.com/news/articles2000/000523-1.shtml

The first half of 2001 had been rough for many E-Commerce companies, and a good number were on the brink of failure. After comprehensively studying the market, the Gartner Group and Consumer Reports are recommending that companies improve their online customer service and policy statements to remain competitive and viable for the future.

Analysts are suggesting that online businesses pay attention to what "bricks and mortar" companies are doing as they enter the online market place. Many are finding the appropriate balance between E-Commerce and traditional business. What E-Commerce retailers must understand is that consumers do not accept the 'pure Web' relationship with the supplier. Consumers need human contact. They need to know that somewhere behind all of the machines, a human is available to assist with site problems and issues.

The Gartner Group recommends steps that E-Commerce retailers can take to improve their business practices ranging from establishing outsourced call centers, to providing consumers foolproof mechanisms for returns. Consumer Reports has stated that basic improvements to E-Commerce websites will improve customer service. According to their studies, most sites could improve ratings from "average" to "excellent" and create a more satisfying online experience by simply clarifying their policy statements. This includes providing excessively complex privacy statements. Online retailers can also improve the usability of their sites by having clear navigation aids and employ a search engine that is flexible. Overall anything that aids the consumer in making a transaction with less hassle certainly helps.

The Marketing Mix

www.ecommercetimes.com/news/articles2000/000208-2.shtml

According to a study by ActivMedia Research, even the most aggressive E-Commerce marketing strategies are unable to compete with the power of brand names and the built-in customer loyalty that they bring. Many consumers buy online from name brands they know and trust offline. Branding is extremely important to consumers when purchasing online.

An increase in traditional mainstream shoppers purchasing on the web occurred in 1999, and again in 2000 . One of the reasons for this increase was the arrival of mainstream companies that are entering E-Commerce full force. The ActivMedia study reports the online fashion and style marketplace, which includes furniture, home and garden, and clothing, generate $4,2 billion in online sales (FY 2000). This, however, only accounted for 1.3 percent of the total spent on these goods. Most online shoppers are loyal repeat customers, and sites must stress customer loyalty. The results of this study revealed that not all online markets are alike, and that not all consumers online are seeking bargains or novelties.

All the marketing efforts in the world, even the best planning marketing mix, cannot take the place of developing a loyal customer base. Other studies, and some prominent companies, argue that the best way to ensure market success is being quick to market, ensuring that you are first. The ActivMedia study refutes that argument, and states that coming to market with a known brand name is more important than getting to market first. Just as it is in the "bricks and mortar" world, long-term success is determined by the customer's opinion of the transaction. Surprising to many, customer service is one of the most important issues in online transactions. Loyal customers are willing to pay more and purchase more line.

Marketers must take into consideration the various characteristics existing in different market segments. Some purchase habitual items while others go online seeking new-look items. It depends on the product category, as well as the type of consumer. For instance, furniture and appliances are two products with highly established brand names that are easily available offline. In this instance, price is the key part of the marketing mix. On the other hand, sporting goods has brand loyalty to particular brands of product instead of particular retailers. Here the product mix must focus on advertising the brand, not the supplier of the product. Generally, the marketing mix is important to E-Commerce retailers. However, they must realize that the brand name is a critical success factor in many sales.

QUESTIONS

1. What are the five steps an E-Commerce retailer can take to improve customer service?
(www.ecommercetimes.com/news/articles2000/000523-1.shtml)

2. Disputing ActivMedia, what do Forrester Research and IBM argue is key for making companies successful online?
(www.ecommercetimes.com/news/articles2000/000208-2.shtml)

3. Why do E-Commerce companies have a hard time using data about consumers?
(http://interactive.wsj.com/public/current/
articles/SB912730671862271500.htm)

CHAPTER 10:
CHANNELS TO MARKET

The Internet has facilitated the creation of three different markets in its short history. The first two are traditional markets of Business-to-Business, and Business-to-Consumer. These two markets, while traditional, are given a new twist on the Internet. The third market is Research Online / Shop Offline. This market captures the individuals that spend time on the Internet researching their purchase, but then go purchase their product offline.

Business-to-Business (B2B)

http://www.ecommercetimes.com/news/articles2000/000721-3.shtml

B2B focuses on all the widgets and gizmos that keep organizations running. The idea is that companies can lower costs by going to Internet mega-sites designed to expedite the purchase of supplies and equipment, instead of having to deal with individual vendors. Virtually every industry has seen the launch of at least one B2B exchange during the past year. Marketplaces are springing up for automakers, Information Technology firms, chemical suppliers, and so forth.

Because industry leaders are concerned with bottom line results, some B2B proponents say, the cost-cutting advantages of the online exchanges will overrule any downside to switching sales channels, such as disrupting long-standing relationships with established vendors. But can the B2B sites reduce prices enough to absorb the costs of building and maintaining their operations—and still charge high enough transaction fees to actualize reasonable profits? Perhaps the critical question is, can they do so before their financial backers lose interest?

Although it moves far more quietly than the much flashier online shopping market, industry analysts, as well as investors, are fixated on the large profit potential of B2B online ventures (**http://www.ecommercetimes.com/news/articles/000104-1.shtml**). The numbers on B2B, however, show its importance. In 1998, analysts estimated that $43 billion (US$) were spent in U.S. online B2B transactions, accounting for only one percent of all B2B commerce in the nation that year. Still, that $43 billion accounted for 84 percent of total E-Commerce revenue. According to Forrester Research (**www.forrester.com**), B2B online revenues will swell to $1.3 trillion over the next three years, while Business-to-Consumer (B2C) E-Commerce revenues will reach only about $108 billion.

B2B operations will likely rely more on long-lasting business relationships and high volume "big kill" transactions. This scenario may best be illustrated by General Motors' alliance with Commerce One, which analysts predict will result in billions of dollars of online transactions with suppliers. B2B will more than occasionally benefit by the "big kill." For example, VerticalNet (**www.verticalnet.com**) , operator of online marketplaces, auctioned off three $38 million dollar power plants in 2000.

E-Commerce analysts are predicting powerful returns for B2B online commerce. According to a new study released by The Boston Consulting Group (**www.bcg.com**) , one-fourth of all U.S. B2B purchasing will be done online by 2003. Further, the study says that today's $700 billion North American B2B E-Commerce market is twice the size of its counterparts in the rest of the world combined ($330 billion).

Business to Consumer (B2C)

http://www.ecommercetimes.com/news/articles2000/000418-1.shtml

U.S. shoppers spent over $61 billion (US$) online in 2000, according to a report by the Boston Consulting Group. The report, entitled "The State of Online Retailing 3.0," was released by Shop.org, a trade association for e-tailers. The data also indicates that the business to consumer (B2C) E-Commerce market will grow 85 percent in following years. In support of this, online automotive sales skyrocketed in 1999, growing 2,300 percent over 1998 sales. Other categories growing at exponential rates included health and beauty at 780 percent, and toys at 440 percent. Total B2C online sales grew 120 percent last year to $33.1 billion—or 1.4 percent of all U.S. retail sales.

A note of caution was issued with the release of the results of a recent Forrester Research report, predicting the imminent demise of most dot-coms (**www.ecommercetimes.com/news/articles2000/000412-7.shtml**). While times ahead promise to be a roller-coaster ride for E-Commerce companies, those companies with a strong consumer focus and an eye toward maximizing profits should emerge unscathed. Major opportunities for growth and profitability have not yet been exploited, according to the report. Specifically, companies could increase revenues by improving their checkout procedures to capture sales from the approximately 65 percent of online shopping carts that are abandoned before customers complete their transactions.

In 1999, more than 75% of B2C sales were in just five industries: computers and computer equipment, travel, brokerage, auction, and books and music (**http://www.emarketer.com/estats/20000719_giga.html**). By 2005, these five will account for only 50%. New categories will make up the difference—auto sales, groceries, toys, gifts, insurance, real estate and government. By 2004, autos and groceries will top online travel and computer sales.

In light of the torrent of anecdotal evidence suggesting that E-Commerce firms may be on the endangered species list, a look at the big picture reveals that the losers inhabit just a small portion of the terrain, and that most inhabitants of the E-Commerce world are not only still breathing, but doing brisk business (**http://www.ecommerce-times.com/news/articles2000/000711-1.shtml**).

As the shakeout runs its inevitable course, some E-tailers are forced to close their virtual doors to their customers. However, those shoppers are not leaving the Internet—they are simply taking their business to other Web sites. Additionally, more new Net stores join the shoppers' ranks every day. Recently, Cambridge, Massachusetts-based Forrester Research found that consumers are increasingly giving E-Commerce a chance (**www.ecommercetimes.com/news/articles2000/000519-1.shtml**). Eleven million more consumers will make purchases online in 2001, driving Internet retail spending to over $38 billion (US$) in the United States. Forrester's research also indicates that Americans are moving from surfing the Web to shopping online at a faster pace than ever before.

Research Online / Purchase Offline

http://www.ecommercetimes.com/news/articles2000/000711-1.shtml

Another important issue is the Internet's influence on offline spending. While some shoppers are not yet confident enough to make purchases online, studies show that preliminary research and comparison shopping on the Internet significantly affect offline purchase decisions.

More than 68 percent of online shoppers said that they researched products online and then made their purchases at a brick and mortar store, according to a Jupiter/NFO Consumer Survey (**http://www.ecommerce-times.com/news/articles2000/000519-1.shtml**). Forty-seven percent said they researched online and then bought over the telephone.

The survey reported that almost 60 percent of wired 16 to 22 year-olds use the Net for research in connection with entertainment spending. While many businesses see their online and offline business as separate sales channels, the report indicates that customers do not make such distinctions. The Jupiter survey also revealed that businesses wanting to succeed in the digital age "must take a broad view of what constitutes success online" and develop an integrated Web presence that allows them to capture and influence both online and offline transactions. Skeptical retailers, eyeing fluctuations in the financial market and the increasing failure rates of Internet companies, are often blind to the most important issue—specifically, the degree to which their online efforts will affect their offline business.

Companies are not doing a good job of tracking the ability of their Web sites to drive sales to traditional channels. The Jupiter Executive survey showed that only 21 percent of multi-channel retailers have the ability to track customers across channels. The retailer that does not understand the impact of the Internet on its store and catalog channels is likely to under-invest in the Internet, missing opportunities to capture incremental sales in all channels.

QUESTIONS

1. What industries stand to gain the most in online B2B commerce over the next three years? (**http://www.ecommercetimes.com/news/articles/000104-1.shtml**)

2. Which industries combined claimed 70% of the B2C market last year? (**http://www.ecommercetimes.com/news/articles2000/000418-1.shtml**)

3. Explain the potential dilemma with B2B transactions. (**http://www.ecommercetimes.com/news/articles2000/000721-3.shtml**)

CHAPTER 11:
STRATEGIC PLANNING FOR
DIRECT CONSUMER
E-COMMERCE

Choosing a Product Line

http://www.cyber-state.org/reportcard.htm

Analysts and historians might long remember Christmas season 1998 as the "coming of age" for World Wide Web-based consumer E-Commerce. Online shoppers pushed consumer-based E-Commerce revenues to almost $8 billion in 1998. Further, analysts are united in the belief that those numbers will continue to grow at a brisk pace for years to come. There are several reasons:

- Choice. Shoppers are no longer limited by how far they can drive. And "shopping bots" are now helping to automate and personalize the online shopping experience, providing exactly what the consumer wants at the lowest possible price.
- Convenience. Online stores never close.
- Better consumer information. The proliferation of online consumer information, such as the dealer costs of new automobiles and self-published consumer comments and reviews, has heightened consumer savvy.

Steadily, these factors are resulting in the masses adopting E-Commerce. Households earning less than $25,000 annually will use sub-$500 Personal Computers and nearly double their share of current online buys from 6 percent to 11 percent in the next few years, according to Forrester Research. As United Parcel Service Chairman and CEO Jim Kelly said in a January 1999 speech before the Economic Club of Detroit, customer preferences now far outweigh retailers' agendas in the buying and selling experience. "How we as corporate managers respond to this new reality will determine our success in the coming decade, and in many cases determine if our businesses will even be around 10 years from now," Kelly said.

At the same time, the Internet offers some of the most powerful direct marketing tools retailers have ever had at their disposal. As the U.S. Department of Commerce (**http://www.doc.gov/**) described in an April 1999 study called "The Emerging Digital Economy," "The Internet offers the opportunity to take direct marketing to the next level: to market directly to narrow bands of customers—even to individuals—and to do so profitably. Amazon.com has taken some first steps in this direction. It greets site visitors by name, informs customers by e-mail when a particular book has arrived or sends them reviews of "best new books" in areas where the customer has indicated an interest. An "instant recommendations" feature proposes books to customers based on purchases they have made at Amazon. Customers can also get an accounting of their purchases at Amazon or see the status of their orders."

The following examples relate how E-Commerce is transforming various consumer-based industries.

In the auto industry, JD Power & Associates estimates that roughly 16 percent of all new car and truck buyers used the Internet as part of their shopping process in 1997, up from 10 percent in 1996. By 2001, they project that the Internet will be used in at least 21 percent of all new car and truck purchases.

In the travel industry, online services are steadily replacing the traditional travel agent. Web-based bookings were more than $800 million in 1997 and are expected to surpass $5 billion by 2001. Polls have indicated that more than two-thirds of Internet users have, or plan to, use online resources to book or research travel.

In the financial services sector, some 22 million U.S. households will have access to online banking and stock trading by 2003, up from 3 million in 1997, according to Forrester Research. Currently, nearly 5 million people actively trade stocks online and pay $8 - $30 per trade (traditional brokerages charge an average of $80 per trade). Investment bank Piper Jaffrey estimates that $614 million in broker commissions were generated online in 1997. This represents more than 4 percent of total retail brokerage commissions and 29 percent of the $2.1 billion in commissions attributable to the discount brokerage sector.

In the insurance industry, Internet-generated premiums are expected to grow from $39 million in 1997 to $1.1 billion by 2001. The rapid increase in sales will be driven by cost savings, increased competition and growing consumer acceptance.

While these overall projections seem astounding at first glance, a closer look reveals the Consumer E-Commerce sector is still very limited in scope. The ten largest retailing web sites account for more than 50 percent of overall retail E-Commerce revenues. Overall, more than 80 percent of retail E-Commerce revenues come from four sectors–computer goods, entertainment, travel, and discount brokerages. And only five percent of web site visitors actually become customers, according to a November 1998 Boston Consulting Group study. The Consumer E-Commerce sector has also been fairly well insulated from major infrastructure problems. A large-scale Internet outage or other unforeseen problems could dampen the positive growth projections.

Choosing a Marketing Format

http://www.att.com/speeches/item/0,1363,2742,00.html#Marketing

An important goal of effective marketing strategy is to reduce the costs of marketing through more accurate targeting of marketing efforts. The Web is virtually tailor-made for this. Both the Web and the closely associated technology of e-mail will eventually provide extraordinary ability to target in both Business-to-Business and Business-to-Customer markets. Internet and e-mail offer outstanding interactivity, comparable to direct sales at a fraction of the cost per contact

Marketing research includes a variety of studies, such as researching various product/market combinations, market potential, market share, sales analysis, and sales forecasting. Typically, the various tools utilized are subheadings of qualitative methods, quantitative methods, and observational studies. Accurately measuring market potential is a critical success factor in determining which target markets are most desirable, the amount of time and money to devote to each, and considering if current sales/advertising/marketing performance is satisfactory (http://www.baclass.panam.edu/mark6371/lectures/research.html).

Perhaps the largest change is taking place in marketing strategy. In the past, a mass-market strategy entailed appealing to the largest number of customers with a single product/marketing program in order to achieve sufficient volumes, economies of scale, and a cost advantage. In contrast, differentiated marketing involves designing separate products/marketing programs for differing segments in anticipation of domination in a particular segment. Deciding the correct method to pursue is essential to success.

Marketing research has been significantly enriched by online communications. Attitudes/beliefs are quicker and easier to test. Dialogues with consumers are easier to maintain, and opinions are easier to record. Costs are minimal to electronically capture these subjects. Visitors to a website are easily tracked regarding number of visits, length of visit, and depth of site penetration, using-measurement software. As a result, traditional media are regarded as read-only type mechanisms, pushing one-way information upon the customer. With the advent of electronic commerce, the interaction is one-to-one, in real-time.

Traditional database and direct-mail marketers could be considered the forerunners of online marketers. They use a set of decision rules attempting to assess the shopper. Since the marketing manager formulated the decision rules, approaches to customize product/service offerings to the consumer are limited to the creativity of the managers. As a result, traditional systems do not fully optimize the consumer's buying power on an individual basis. Online electronic commerce, collaborative filtering, and online databases are increasingly becoming the methods of choice.

Collaborative filtering involves learning from each customer interaction, in real time, to adjust marketing and/or product offering to meet the unique needs and preferences of a particular customer. This technology, popularized through its use on Amazon.com's website, began in 1968 when the global publishing industry developed the ISBN (International Standard Book Number) system. The unique labeling system of each book combined with FireFly software agent technology, allows the examination of a pool of customer purchases via ISBN, then extending online customized offerings to each individual in a real-time venue.

Marketing managers can use collaborative filtering in applications, other than books, to leverage the power of consumers visiting a website to enable them to determine future product offering. The application of the technology is usually designed to meet the needs of a particular vertical industry. As a result, collaborative filtering software packages may not work well across diverse industries. In addition, online offerings that result from a collaborative filtering software program are based upon assumptions of buyer similarity. Companies in particular industries avoid online offerings to sole customers based upon other customers serving as surrogates for that particular buyer online at a given point in time.

Since many companies have older, offline databases and new market offerings online, the issue of integrating both systems is arduous. The ability to access more data regarding past and present customers preferences and purchase histories is powerful. Integrating the old systems with the new web software in a different language is difficult. However, for traditional companies establishing an online presence, with website, and electronic commerce capabilities, the sooner they synchronize, the sooner they will have a sustainable advantage over their dot-com only competitors.

According to Jonathon Brookner, director of One-to-One Research at Peppers and Rogers Group, a Stamford, Connecticut-based strategic marketing firm, "Customers want to be able to order something online and then go to a retail store if it needs to be exchanged." Without synchronizing online and offline databases, the task would be impossible.

Synchronization would also help resolve channel conflict resulting from manufacturer online offerings of small orders or replacement parts filled by the manufacturer. With a synchronized database, the larger orders are easily passed along to regional dealers.

A major advantage of synchronized online/offline databases, for firms with traditional storefronts and an electronic commerce website, is the ability to capture customer e-mail addresses at the traditional storefront, then use them for e-mail marketing campaigns. Williams-Sonoma, a home retailing giant based in San Francisco, implements this method. Their response rate for the first e-mail marketing campaign was a tremendous 11 percent coupon redemption rate, as opposed to the typical 1-2 percent offline, direct-mail marketing campaigns. Market analysis capabilities of any company with a traditional and online presence would be significantly enhanced by a synchronized online/offline database.

Due to the relative infancy of electronic commerce, the rapid growth of personal computer sales and Internet use, it is a nebulous task to utilize a single component of online or offline market research/analysis techniques with low relative risk. In a rapidly changing industry, market analysis results may be outdated in a short period of time. In light of all of the aforementioned issues, the combination of market analysis methods, with those methods used online and offline, would offer the best options for future consumers. Electronic marketing offers the speed, low cost, and relative high quality of online market analysis methods (http://www.baclass.panam.edu/mark6371/lectures/research.html).

Knowing your Competition

http://www.score.org/faqs/business/faq1b.html

Very few businesses operate in a vacuum, i.e., without competition in a specific market. There also may be indirect competition, which has a significant impact on customer's buying decisions in the marketplace. Direct and non-direct competitors are trying to convince customers to buy their product rather than yours. It is in one's best interest to attempt to know more about the companies that are trying to earn one's business. To start, list the strengths and weaknesses of each of your competitors. Talk with colleagues, visit the competition, call for information about their products and analyze how they advertise. Next, list each of the major competitors and rate each, using a scale of 1 to 10, for product quality, process, advertising and customer satisfaction. Add other ratings that are deemed important.

Use this competitive analysis to make decisions in concerning the strategic marketing plan, which is an integral part of the business plan. Knowing the competition enables one to gain a competitive advantage, which may result in mores sales and profits. The marketing plan will provide guidance towards the right decisions in the areas of pricing and advertising. It will also lead the firm to gain an advantage in customer satisfaction. Finally, it might also assist in making the right decision in other areas of the marketing plan, such as customer and product segmentation. In summary, it is impossible to produce a realistic marketing plan and business plan, without knowing one's competition.

QUESTIONS

1. Why would analysts and historians long remember Christmas season 1998 as the "coming of age" for World Wide Web-based consumer E-Commerce? (**http://www.cyber-state.org/reportcard.htm**)

2. Why has marketing research been significantly enriched by online communications?
(**http://www.baclass.panam.edu/mark6371/lectures/research.html**).

3. What are the key points in the Michigan state report card on E-Commerce?
http://www.cyber-state.org/reportcard.htm

CHAPTER 12:
INTERNET STRATEGY AND
IMPLEMENTATION

As organizations migrate from geographically-based infrastructures to virtual global organizations, personnel and information process systems must change to capitalize on the opportunity. Jobs will no longer be duplicated (in geographical sectors) to conduct simple tasks such as sales, order processing and logistical functions. As new computer systems and data exchange mechanisms are created using universal coding systems such as Sun's Java code, firms have increased opportunities to link closer to the customers. However, before an Internet strategy can be implemented, the Internet strategy team must understand the five main processes for an Internet based business strategy: On-line Store Front, Payment Processing, Shipping/Order Fulfillment, Customer Service, and Promotion. Each of these five separate functions provides the foundation of a proper Internet commerce strategy (**http://www.ecommerce.about.com/smallbusiness/ecommerce/librar y/weekly/aa030600a.htm**).

Digital Supply Chain Analysis

http://www.thesupplychain.com/tscm/

Regardless of the apparent media glamorization of marketing and advertisement, and the "exciting allure" of an Internet based company for potential IPO investors, the successful business truly defines what makes it unique—its sustainable, competitive advantage against all competitors. The company must be sharply focused in this area to maintain a competitive advantage at all times, as globalization trends continually pressure prices downward. This is especially true in the U.S. economy over the last six years, due to global competition and the strong U.S. dollar exchange rate.

The strong currency attracts weaker currency countries to participate in the marketplace. Regardless of currency exchange issues or global supply impacts, as corporations migrate their business strategies to Web based B2B or B2C business models, the need for traditional sales, order processing and credit management services disappear. They are replaced by new employment opportunities for logistical support, IT support, and the development of interpersonal relationships between vendors and customers.

The first step for implementing a virtual business strategy is to complete a digital supply chain analysis. This must be balanced against the existing supply chain model, and the strength and weaknesses must be compared. Next, the projected industry changes over three to five years must be determined, discovering new market size potential and value in order to determine market needs. Third, a digital value chain analysis must be conducted to determine if the new business strategic goals and methodology are realistic. Finally, if the value obtained by this model is in line with organizational goals and industry expectations, then the business strategy is ready for implementation. Special care must be taken to implement the changes while maintaining focus on the core business externally, as the organization modifies to a new mode of business. However, if the projected digital value chain model does not produce realistic business expectations, or is out of line with industry's expectations, then the entire process needs to be re-evaluated. For example, if consumers expectations from a product are extremely low prices and limited to no technical support, then an organization must remove infrastructure that does not support the marketplace value on the goods and services provided by the organization. The digital value chain analysis must encompass a reverse auctioning process, purchasing orders, requisitioning, invoicing, fulfillment and logistics, catalog, inventory management, demand planning and materials requirements planning.

Global Marketplace Strategy

http://ecommerce.about.com/gi/dynamic/offsite.htm?site=http://www.cf.ac.uk/uwcc/masts/ecic/eleccomm.html

1999 E-Commerce sales globally accounted for $145 billions dollars, and by 2004 the projected global should reach $7.3 trillion dollars. Business cannot afford to ignore the value of the Internet, especially as emerging markets continue to grow and stabilize in the economy. However to ensure that business growth continues, a large concern must be resolved—security, or lack there of. Three key aspects of any Web-based business strategy must involve value-laden content, enhanced search capabilities within the web site, and a simplified buying process. If implemented correctly, each of these aspects can be far less expensive in terms of costs than traditional means in the old economy business model.

As the global marketplace offers new opportunities to most businesses, caution must be advised when dealing in commerce in foreign lands. Some governments regulate information availability and impose tariffs on "generic product names." For example, China has an additional 3.5 percent tariff, in addition to other tariffs and taxes, on any product associated with nutrition. Dog food, paper plates, plastic eating utensils are included in this category. If taxes are not properly obtained by the seller at the point of sale, then the seller is responsible at a later date, typically when goods and services are withheld due to unpaid taxes. Other issues regarding the global growth of the Internet include the lack of public infrastructure, various government laws regarding point of sale material and labeling, and the limited bandwidths available in foreign markets. Fortunately, the global marketplace via the Internet is in its early stages, allowing most business entities the chance to modify strategies in time to reap the rewards of the virtual global economy.

From Business Vision to Strategic Plan Implementation
http://www.cf.ac.uk/masts/ecic/eleccomm.html

Once the company's strategic development team has clearly defined the business strategy and established strengths and weakness against the competition, then the organization can determine what the real market size is and what techniques it will use to obtain its market share. After this vision is developed, the virtual business model can quickly assess the customer's needs and incorporate them into the virtual model. For example, many large multinational organizations desire instant access to information about their suppliers concerning business areas such as: (1) how much (in overall dollar terms and measurement units) they have purchased from a supplier; (2) how many products are purchased globally; and (3) what are their outstanding orders in units measured and overall dollar terms. This is typically unique to the large multinationals, but many medium sized organizations want to know the status of their orders, when it is scheduled to arrive, and what stage of order fulfillment the supplier is at in time. All of these answers can be obtained by properly designing the virtual web based community to ensure both the company's internal and external needs are met, by linking valued customers and suppliers together prior to designing the business system.

As information transfers among various companies within a product's value chain, the need for seamless transmission of information becomes a critical success factor. Thus, companies, supplier, and target customers must be linked together to maximize the return for all parties. As one United Kingdom CEO stated, "its no good in being the worlds finest company, if in fact you have lousy supplier and weak customers." This statement is extremely powerful and all levels of management must come to the realization that once an electronic network system is established among customers and vendors, many once-private issues on sales and operational planning, inventory management, cash flow, or any other business issue could become exposed to the customers and vendors. Thus, proper design and management is critical in this new business model, ensuring that all business systems are designed with the end customer in mind.

The electronic commerce model must address infrastructure requirements, marketing, educational mechanisms, and payment systems. The final link could be the most critical in the strategic model development: implementation of the strategic Internet plans, including timelines and objectives criteria. Too often, excessive energy is spent designing the perfect plan only to be passed along for others to implement and live with. This type of approach leads to failure and non-commitment from different groups within the organization. To ensure the business remains focused, first employ an expert to design and implement the business model. If an internal expert is not available, outsource a professional project manager. Once the strategy has been established for a market sector, create a cross-functional business team to lead the development and implementation of the project. This aspect should have several iterations throughout various phases of the project, but done in different stages, and established by the project manager. An additional benefit accrued is the creation of product champions to assist with both communication to, and education of, others within their department concerning the project. This may sound basic, but simple steps in modifying organizational infrastructure can cause dramatic conflicts if not communicated properly and professionally. Once the web site is up and running, time must be allocated to ensure everyone, in all business aspects, is aware of the site and has an opportunity to see it. This extra communication establishes pride within the group, company, and organization because most employees realize that the Internet is an important piece of any future business strategy. This added communication channel allows all members of an organization to feel their organization is moving toward the future in a positive way (**http://www.cf.ac.uk/masts/ecic/netcom.html**).

QUESTIONS

1. List services and benefits accrued from using an online shipping provider for E-Commerce shipping needs. (**http://www.ecommerce.about.com/gi/dynamic/offsite.htm?site=http://www.iship4u.com**)

2. Briefly describe how the Internet can be leveraged to improve the supply chain. (**http://www.thesupplychain.com/tscm/**)

3. List a number of dominant industries that have incorporated E-Commerce into their existing businesses and how this has impacted their existing businesses. (**http://www.cf.ac.uk/masts/ecic/netcom.html**)

CHAPTER 13:
ELECTRONIC PAYMENT

Due the complex level of successful business models available for use in the global economy, there is no single E-Commerce solution to any problem or set of problems. However, by having a clearly focused strategy to maximize exposure and sales revenue using the E-Commerce model, businesses can dramatically increase sales revenues. Each business model is different and will vary, depending on the range of products and services it provides and the method it delivers those products and services to the end consumer. A value chain analysis should be conducted and validated before developing any E-Commerce business model to ensure a design that will maximize the value delivered to consumers. This chapter outlines a variety of business models, based on the size of the organization.

Small Business Requirements

http://www.ecommerce.about.com/smallbusiness/ecommerce/library/weekly/aa030600a.html

The allure of global potential sales and exponentially reaching new customers is exciting to many small, regional based companies. In addition, with relatively low start up costs to reach these global communities, as compared to the old economy ways of setting up regional offices and hiring agents to service your customers, some firms become so enticed by the allure of the new business venture, the expansion needs are given inadequate consideration. Many times the failures of successful regional and small national companies have resulted from improper infrastructure to sustain business needs, as they migrated to a virtual, global marketplace. Thus before conducting business on the web, a company should first define what it wants the web to bring to the business.

Online Stores offer a business model that can literally be plugged into most small business infrastructures. This model employs the virtual store front window, where consumers can purchase goods and services. This type of model may not be a good fit where services are typically custom designed and manufactured. However for most small businesses, reaching their consumers is critical, and this model literally levels the playing field between a small "mom and pop" operation verses a large multinational organization—without the end consumer knowing the difference.

A payment option must be tailored to meet the business needs, typically if the business model for the online store is B2C. A credit card or on-line checking payment system is required for goods and service to be shipped. Several providers of such services exist, ranging from turnkey to integrated web designs. Credit cards are by far the most common means of transferring funds; however, new systems such as *ibill.com*, (**http://www.ibill.com/onlinechecks.html**) provide new online checking accounts, and these are growing in popularity. This system is less expensive than credit card transactions, involves less on-line players, and due to less communication requirements to complete a transaction, is typically faster. The *ibill.com* system pays merchants for online check sales twice a month, on a fifteen day rolling basis. Another feature of *ibill.com* is that consumers, who have either exceeded their existing credit card limit, or who are new Internet users, can immediately use this service without going through the long verification process of Smart Cards. However, as with all new systems, there are negative aspects. Of particular mention is the wide use of credit card debit and the limited number of western hemisphere consumers, who actually pay for items on cash basis from their checking accounts.

Any small business model must determine how the firm will design its new reach of channels-to-markets design. Many regional and small national firms utilize internal shipping and handling systems. Obviously this is not practical for the global aspect of the new sales possibilities, thus a Federal Express, UPS, DHL, or similar type of global shipping network must be utilized. UPS and Federal Express have plug and play web based designed systems that can be incorporated directly into the Small Business website handling both the payment and the shipping direction. This simplifies the process for many companies, in that UPS collects the payment from the payer and UPS pays the Small Business (less fees of service). This simple system allows small companies to combine shipping and billing solutions. However, there are also negative aspects with this model as well, particularly when a merchant loses some contact with customers. Another negative aspect is that potentially credit risk consumers can be rejected by the UPS online credit system, which may be perceived as a reflection on the small company, not UPS.

Complex Business Models Requirements

http://www.verifone.hp.com/corporate_info/press?rel?html/pr033099_ips.html

Small regional businesses, looking to increase their sales distribution systems, may use the options provided by the vast number of electronic commerce payment organizations, such as Creditservice International, Verifone.com, UPS.com, or ccnow.com, which can immediately handle most common invoicing needs, domestically. These services are not inexpensive—typical fees can range between 8 to12 percent of the total sales revenues, in addition to the credit card charge fees. For a small business, this extra expense for value added services can typically be absorbed by the few number of online orders, coupled with the additional sales revenue generated from the web based business. These extra costs may adversely impact profits if the sales volume is high.

Outsourcing this critical business function can be beneficial to a start-up organization. As the company grows, often these outsourced resources can be crippling to the profit margins of an organization, especially one with a large infrastructure. A good example is the outsourcing of one's credit department for the E-Commerce website sales. Often an outside source can have different business expectations and limitations that are contrary to the business unit's expectation and market place conditions. In addition, the vendor may process several hundreds of orders a day, via EDI, facsimile and/or via telephone call centers. Thus, the large multinational organizations must link their web based order processing functions into the existing firm's infrastructure to maximize synergistic benefits. These linked requirements demand that each Internet business model be somewhat customer designed to both fit the business model, as well be compatible with the business computer systems.

Hewlett-Packard's Verifone offers a variety of services to meet consumers demanding needs. Verifone's plug and play web based systems are designed to operate under the Window NT server network and can be incorporated behind the web site browser as a supporting tool. Verifone is a global leader in providing secure electronic payment solutions for three separate categories: web based merchants, consumers, and financial institutions, which service the web for electronic payments. Types of software designs that would be integrated into a merchant's existing order processing system include:

Electronic Wallet

(http://www.verifone.hp.com/solutions/internet/vwallet/index.ht ml)

An Electronic Wallet is a software program that stores a customer's information on their own desktop, eliminating the need to continually refresh information such as customer name, shipping, and billing address, and payment information. Electronic wallets support a variety of credit cards, digital cash, paper and digital checking accounts, and blanket purchase orders (coupled with letters of credit). This type of system only requires a buyer to click on the "buy" icon to place an order (**http://www.processing.net/info.html**).

Merchant Register

(http://www.verifone.hp.com/solutions/internet/vpos/html/solution.html). A merchant register is a type of software links a merchant to a credit card service or financial service provider in order to exchange payment for services rendered. Typically these software packages include support for SET and SSL types of security protocols between the consumer, merchant, and financial provider. Cybercash.com, eTill.com, and Verifone.com are the largest suppliers of these types of software packages. The design costs and the maintenance fees to support the system are dependent upon the complexity of the merchant's computer system network.

Financial Institution

(http://www.verifone.hp.com/solutions/internet/vgate/index.html). This organization contracts with the merchant to enable the acceptance, processing, and deposit of credit card transactions. Merchants are required to maintain an account with a financial institution to receive credit for credit card sales. Establishing an account with a financial institution is uncomplicated. Simply contact the institution, describe your E-Commerce configuration, and select an Internet payment service such as; First Data Corporation, Global Payment Systems, or Nova Information Systems. These organizations provide billing, customer support, government reporting, authorization and collection services for merchants for on-line credit transactions.

Designing a Generic Payment Service Model

http://www.research.ibm.com/journal/sj/371/abadpeiro.html

Due to the complexity of integrating "bolt-on" Web based order-processing systems that allow for electronic commerce for business, several companies have designed base line generic payment systems that can replace a merchant order processing system. These systems are developed with universal computer code systems, such as Java, to ensure a variety of networks will readily integrate the data. Ironically almost every order processing model holds its internal order processing data uniquely to its internal needs and therefore cannot be integrated into other systems without going through a data gateway or warehouse system. These systems must be updated daily and, when in operation, can dramatically slow down or freeze the overall order entry system. Most consumers, while placing an order have heard the phrase, "...the system for some reason is slow today." These types of delays typically are caused by the enormous activity between the data warehouses, the hold on order processing systems, and the "original" order process system. Also if any one of these systems has an error or breaks down, then the entire system shuts down.

Many organizations, when migrating to an E-Commerce business model, will completely redesign the order process and payment systems.

The new systems tend to obtain the order in four separate models: telephone, facsimile, Electronic data Interchange (EDI), and web based commerce. The system then moves the order into a common template, transferring the electronic value from a payer to a payee, and reverses order for payment of services. In the simplest form, this interaction will only take place between two electronic points, such as merchant and financial entity. For example, the financial entity performs a service for the merchant and gets paid. As the system transactions become more complicated, such as international shipments and currency rate balances, the more modularized the generic payment system will become. The overall benefit of these types of universal "generic" code systems are that as the business model changes, the system can change without migrating the order process data from its existing field of operations.

QUESTIONS

1. Explain how an online checking service, such as Ibill.com functions and provides benefits to both users and its customers.
(http://www.ibill.com/onlinechecks.html)

2. What is a growing important need of electronic commerce and what are developers doing to overcome this dilemma?
(http://www.research.ibm.com/journal/sj/371/abadpeiro.html)

3. Explain how an online electronic payment service, such as Authorized.net can improve the ability to collect payments from electronic commerce sales.

(Hint: there are 13 potential benefits, only list the key areas for your business needs)
(**http://ecommerce.about.com/gi/dynamic/offsite.htm?site=http%3A%2F%2Fwww.authorizenet.com%2F**)

Chapter 14:
AUCTION TECHNOLOGY

As technology changes over time, new business opportunities often follow, presenting opportunities to the public. One example of this concept is the revitalization of the auction industry, an old standard for the selling of expensive property such as antiques, paintings, bankruptcy/liquidation, or real estate. Now, through the ability of the Internet reaching a global community linked to the world wide web, the auction process has been revitalized. Today, the industry of online auctions is one of the fastest growing areas of the Internet. eBay has more than five million users and features more than 2.5 million products for sale 365 days a year, twrnty-four hours a day (**http://www.butterfields.com/index2.html**).

At the beginning of the 20th century, the auction process was limited to bankruptcy liquidation sales, or estate sales. However, with today's technology of the World Wide Web, virtually anyone in the world has access to the bidding process in a virtual auction. Online auction categories include topics such as antiques, movies, coins, pottery, sports memorabilia, toys, etc. (**http://www.hypermart.net/members/tutorials/101/questionaire.gsp**).

Almost any item can be sold or purchased online through an auction process. Recently, eBay officials halted the bidding process of the following items: a human kidney, future brides from Russia, and potential money laundering schemes. In this revitalized industry, goods are posted via a description and electronic image of the product. A bidding period is set for the virtual auction to begin. Today, approximately 10 percent of all E-Commerce transactions come from an auction process (**http://pages.ebay.com/community/aboutebay/overview/index.html**).

Auction processes allow potential customers to determine the price of the item being sold via the open market policy, which determines the true value of the product. In addition to obtaining true market value, this process can dramatically reduce distribution costs. Instead of goods being shipped from regional warehouses and inventory held for customer demand, the auction process allows for distribution centers to be centrally located in a single location, with freight being handled on an individual order basis. An ancillary benefit is the reduction of surplus inventory. This system allows a manufacturer to quickly remove excess inventory that would normally sit "on the books" until it was devalued to market value and sold as a sale item.

Typically, this process involves advertisement for liquidation sales, as well as extra sales staff support. However, with the auction process, this is an ongoing activity to better manage the cash flow position. Often, the auction profit per item is lower than utilizing a traditional market channel. If the net present value is weighed, typically the auction process is much more profitable for the company, especially if large inventory is held for a long period.

Types of Auctions

http://interiordec.about.com/gi/dynamic/offsite.htm?site=http://www.butterfields.com/buy/buyterms.html
http://www.business-auctions.com/help/bidder.html

The auctioning process has extended beyond the B2C model. Encrypted technology allows for multiple participants within the same industry to share the benefits of bundled purchases from their vendors, in turn selling opportunities to their customers, without having to share the details with each partner. Thus the B2B business model has now become an active system for many large multinational organizations, which want to leverage both their buying decision as well as their selling position to the industry. Numerous large industries, such as automotive, shipping/long freight carriers, textile, food companies, power, and software providers are starting to bundle their purchases within a closed auction system, to both their suppliers and customers. Three types of auction methods are employed to obtain bids: Open Cry, Sealed Bid, or Dutch Rules.

- **Open Cry Auction.** This is the most common type of auction, where the highest bidder purchases the product. This process starts the bidding at a low price and continues to offer more money for an item until the final minute on the last day of bidding. This type of process is excellent for products that perspective buyers can afford the time to place counter bids throughout the specified period and feel comfortable about making counter offers within a few minutes or hours. This type of auction works well for antiques, books and tickets
  (**http://www.theonlinemarket.com/types.html**).

- **Sealed Bid Auction.** A sealed bid implies that a bidder for the product is not aware of the other bidder's information, such as their names and how much they are offering. Sealed bid auctions are practiced when it is not possible for the bidders to prepare counter bids efficiently. Typically, companies do not like to reveal their competitors bid information to other vendors. All government based bid proposals are done this way. It is the seller's advantage to keep the bid private until the auction is completed
  (**http://www.goverment-auctions.com/fedga2.htm**).

- **Dutch Auction.** This process similar to the open cry auction style, but instead of starting the process at zero and working up, this process starts at the highest bid price, and the bid is decreased until the first customer bids for the good. This shifts the market price control from a buyer's market, to a suppliers market in that they control the bid price level and ultimately the price of the goods. This is a quick bid process, and is a benefit to most suppliers in that their prices can be higher than a traditional open cry auction. (**http://www.boardline.com/sellers/sellertips.cfm**)

Auction Markets

http://www.findarticles.com/cf_1/M0CXD_1999_DEC/59479431/PR INT/HTML

EBay, Amazon.com, Yahoo!, and Priceline.com are popular web sites that have exploited the public attention concerning auction technology. Most of this auction activity is for a B2C business model. These auctions resemble a virtual garage sale, when one considers the variety of merchandise and the diversity of participants. A Forester Research report indicated that consumer to consumer online auctions generated $120 million dollars of revenue in 1998 and had grown to $19 billion dollars by 2000. Besides different types of auctions, different types of business models exist for each auction process.

- **Consumer to Consumer Business Model Auction** (**http://www.agorics.com/auctions/auction1.html**). Most auction services currently service this market, Consumer to Consumer, where goods and services are provided for individuals. EBay created this market by illustrating a large demand for this type of activity existed. EBay sustained an average growth rate in asset value of 210% annually, for its first five years of existence (http://www.ebay.com/community/aboutebay/overview/index.h tml). This style of auction does not dictate how the final payment should be made. These types of online auction markets allow the buyer and seller to negotiate payment methods and shipping details. To prevent fraud in these types of transactions, companies, such as I-escrow, will hold the buyers money in an escrow account until the good is received by the buyer, then forward the money to the seller (less a processing fee of 1.5 percent of the selling price) (http://www.agorics.com/auctions/auction1.html).

The Consumer to Consumer process works well because participants become excited during the bidding process, develop a sense of urgency as auctions close, and enjoy the potential for a bargain. Each auction company charges for services rendered in different ways. Yahoo! does not charge for online auction services, but generates profits via selling advertisements, due to the large amount of web traffic generated. Priceline.com purchases large number of popular airline tickets in bulk from the airlines, then proceeds to sell them to the public as the bid process begins. The difference between the buying price and selling price is the profit for Priceline.com (http://www.priceline.com/PricelineASPHomepage/asp/company.asp?session_key=D00011ACD10011AC2000083112231904207170705 8   ). Ebay and Amazon charge a fee to the seller for offering this service; they also offer additional features and services which are charged above their standard fee of 5 percent selling price, coupled with a fixed fee for the website service/maintenance fee.

Business to Consumer Auctions (http://www.gpbid.com/).
This process typically revolves around liquidation of excess inventory. Repeat site visits by customers have been extremely high (65 percent) when compared to other forms of advertisements and promotion.

Consumers often perceive they are receiving a better value by buying direct from the manufacturer instead of going through a various network of logistical and warehouse systems. A downside is the cost associated with these small orders, in comparison to the traditionally large orders most manufacturers enjoy. To ensure that the auction process does not interfere with traditional market offerings and prevent price erosion to other markets, many manufactures re-label existing product line offerings (to prevent direct comparison, or change the package size).

Business to Business Auction
(http://www.teksell.com/buyerservice.cfm). This is potentially the largest market for the online auction process business model. In this business model, companies approve a variety of suppliers and place bid offers on their websites. Approved suppliers offer bids for the business, and the buyer decides which company will get the business. As a second variation, a supplier places an offering on a series of buyer websites for a product offering and price. For example, a vendor-approved computer supplier could contact a large manufacturer and indicate they have 25 computers for sale at $250.00 each, as long as the company purchases all of the computers at one time. This offer can be sent to a variety of companies, in attempt to move the product. Whichever company responds first receives the low price for these computers. Other business models have been developed, which sell government surplus items on line **(http://www.financenet.gov/financenet/sales/sales.htm**).

Infrastructure Requirements

http://www.netmerchants.com/products/auctioneer/lite.asp

Several different technology suppliers, meeting customer needs from turnkey operations to custom designed systems or components, are used to implement auction technology for any of the three different auction business models. Vendors such as Microsoft, Netmerchants, Opensite Technology, and IBM are the largest vendor suppliers for auction technology solutions. Each vendor offers a different scenario for solutions and benefits, depending upon infrastructure capabilities and auction requirements. These range in complexity from a consumer looking to clear out a garage, to the selling of rare and exotic items (**http://www.netmerchants.com/products/auction-eer/merchant.asp**). If a company wishes to incorporate E-Commerce business models into existing Windows-based software systems, options are available that can meet both large and small business needs. The following are some of the more popular web based sites that offer E-Commerce solutions. Each solution offers a different technique to gain access to an auction process. The good news for auction technology is that this marketplace is rapidly expanding. Sales of E-Commerce auction systems surpassed $400 million in 1999, up from $58 million in 1998.

- **Microsoft (http://www.microsoft.com/customers/details.asp?solid=3566)** has developed an auction component that supports three types of auctions: winning bid, clear price and second price. A winning bid allows winning customers to receive the item for set price determined between organizations. A clear auction process rewards bidders when there are multiple items for sale and goal it so all winning bidders pay the same price. In a second price auction, each winning customer pays the lowest of the following: the highest losing bid plus the bid increment, the lowest winning bid, or the reserve price. Microsoft.com solutions are typically used for the high-end user, who desires to have tremendous web traffic and integrate their web auction service into existing Windows NT server infrastructure.

- **Netmerchants (http://www.auctioneer32.com**) offer an easy to use auctioneer software package designed for business to consumer or consumer to consumer auctions. The software provides control over the bidding process, defining bid increments and specific payment types. The software includes templates and configuration files for managing all aspects of E-Commerce needs. These software systems are affordable and excellent for small business users

- **Opensite Technologies (http://www.opensite.com/osa.htm**) offers auction packages for all aspects of the auction process: B2B, B2C, C2B and C2C. All of their software packages utilize the Microsoft explorer technology base and can be universally accepted with its web browser Java coding. Opensite.com offers true plug and play software solutions that, within a few hours, can have auction capabilities up and running.

- **IBM (http://www.research.ibm.com/rules/home.html**) offers software packages that can be operated on both Windows-based platforms and Macintosh systems. It offers an open cry, sealed bid, and Dutch auction styles with the ability to create reserve prices, information available to the bidders only, and tie breaking rules. Geographical restrictions, starting/ending dates and time frames can be defined. Terms of payment are available to the merchant looking to sell products in an auction format. IBM's software offers a unique package that is either self contained on a Windows NT or Windows 2000 platform, or it can be run from a server based on the IBM Net.commerce licensed software. These systems manage both the web activity and the E-Commerce activity (**http://www-4.ibm.com/software/web-servers/commerce/servers/wcsver4.html**).

QUESTIONS

1. Discuss three options a seller must decide upon in a reverse-e-auction process.
(**http://www.findarticles.com/cf_0/m3148/10_128/62775003/p1/article.jhtml**)

2. Why are existing large suppliers reluctant to enter the E-Commerce marketplace?
(**http://www.findarticles.com/cf_0/m3148/10_128/62775003/p1/article.jhtml**)

3. List ten tips for purchasing a "bargain" via an online auction.
(**http://www.findarticles.com/cf_0/m0CXD/1999_Dec/59479431/p5/article.jhtml**)

CHAPTER 15:
FUTURE OF E-COMMERCE

Several projections have been made concerning the future of E-Commerce. These projections typically fall into one of two categories: usage or technology. Two new technologies currently being discussed are wireless applications to reach the Internet, and Digital TV. These technologies are discussed in this chapter, along with a projection of internet usage for the future.

Wireless Applications

http://www.ecmgt.com/Jun2000/management.perspective.htm

The potential opportunities for wireless applications opportunity seem limitless. The number of Internet-enabled mobile devices will exceed the number of personal computers by 2003, with the Gartner Group estimating more than one billion mobile devices in use by that date. By 2004, more than 30 percent of all wireless users will access the Internet through mobile devices. Dollars spent on mobile E-Commerce services will rise to over $200 billion in 2005.

Mobile commerce, known as M-Commerce, is gradually arriving in the United States. With experts predicting one billion Web-enabled mobile phones in use by 2003, these devices will be the most common method used to reach the Internet, as well as conduct E-Commerce. M-Commerce growth rates are projected to increase 100 percent per year, and by 2003, the wireless E-business market will reach $66 billion dollars.

M-Commerce will work best in areas that emphasize the core virtues of wireless networks: convenience, personalization, and location. The driving force behind this is the idea that putting the Internet in the "palm of the hand" will give business professionals, and consumers alike, ever-increasing access to data and information, forcing E-business and web commerce strategists to rethink and redesign their E-business process. Growth of M-Commerce will require alliances among large telecommunications firms, financial services providers, and content providers.

Consumer services include one-way notification for news, sports, weather, and stock quotes. Typical transactions include credit and debit card payments through cell phones, shopping for music, books, and theatre tickets, and most importantly, stock market trading. It is estimated that by 2004, half of all day stock trades will be conducted from mobile phones.

Mobile marketing is also a very interesting niche–because consumers will personalize their (wireless) portal to receive only the kind of information they want, creating a very powerful driver for one to one marketing. Mobile operators can track calling patterns, and with eventual precision in positioning technology, will know where users are any time of the day. Can you envision "instant ice cream discounts" when you're within a mile of Baskin Robbins?

Digital TV

http://www.ecommercetimes.com/news/articles2000/000320-1.shtml

For the average consumer, the phrase "Digital TV" conjures up images of crystal clear pictures and ear-popping sound. In actuality, however, the technology promises more than just enhancements to the audio-visual experience—it will allow a greater and more diverse population around the world to participate in the Internet Age.

Digital TV will do far more than show television in a digital format. The term actually describes a series of interrelated technologies that will allow television to become interactive, so that viewers can play along with game shows, get information from the Internet as they watch a show, or buy a vast array of products and services online.

The implications are enormous. E-Commerce companies will finally be able to reach consumers who are unable or unwilling to buy a personal computer. E-Commerce will also turn the TV into an instant procurement machine. Interactive television will not require the purchase of new systems. Existing television sets will simply require an attached device that will receive the digital signals from broadcasters or from the Internet, and translate those to analog signals.

Digital television can be subdivided into three closely related models of operation. The first model, called "single mode," allows the viewer to switch between the television program and the interactive application. When the viewer finishes the interactive activity, he or she returns to regular viewing. In the second model, known as "simultaneous mode," the viewer "pops-up" the interactive application into a picture-in-picture (PIP) window on the television screen and is able to interact while continuing to watch the program. For example, a viewer would be able to answer questions along with the contestants on a quiz show. The third model, or "pause mode," records television programs to a hard disk, thereby allowing viewers to pause the program in order to use the full screen to take advantage of the interactive service. When the interaction is over, viewers can continue the program at the point where it was paused.

By 2006, the E-Commerce Times predicts virtually every person who uses the Internet will also use interactive television. While PC-based E-Commerce revenues are expected to grow to $105 billion in 2006, TV-based E-Commerce is expected to match that figure. The major growth is expected to take place in 2005 and 2006, as interactive digital TV products and services begin to dominate Internet activity.

While the projections are made for the U.S. only, E-Commerce on interactive television will have an enormous impact on a worldwide level. The impact, however, must be considered on a country by country basis, taking into account the various regulations associated with television advertising. In countries that have similar policies to the U.S., E-Commerce via interactive television will likely equal or exceed PC-based E-Commerce by the mid-2000's. In nations that restrict TV advertising, however, the impact will be less pronounced.

Potential Size of E-Commerce

http://www.ecommercetimes.com/news/articles2000/000712-7.shtml

According to a report released by New York-based eMarketer (www.eMarketer.com), three of four Internet users will be shopping online by 2003, and 68 percent of all U.S. Web users will be online shoppers by the end of 2001. The study, entitled *eConsumer Shopping Report*, also predicts that U.S. revenues from online shopping will reach $37 billion (US$) by year-end 2001 and will grow to $104 billion in 2003. "E-Commerce growth will be driven primarily by new users and buyers for the next few years. After 2003, however, most growth will come from increased spending per individual user or Internet-using household," said eMarketer Senior Analyst Darren Allen.

The results of the survey revealed that almost 34 million U.S. households are actively using the Internet, and purchases have been made in 23.5 million U.S. households. By 2003, eMarketer predicts that 52 million households will be online and more than 42 million households will be shopping online. Correspondingly, the number of individual Americans shopping online is set to increase from 63.4 million by the end of 2001, to 106 million by 2003.

Not only will more Americans be shopping online in the coming years, the results of the survey also indicated that they will be spending more. By the end of 2001, the average Internet buyer will purchase $627 worth of goods online, up from $500 in 1999. By 2003, the number is expected to reach $1,033.

Confirming a report released by Greenfield Online (**www.greenfield.com**) detailing Internet use by senior citizens, eMarketer predicts that older users are entering the Web in ever increasing numbers, and are expected to become the second-largest untapped customer base after minorities.

A study released by The Boston Consulting Group revealed that 25 percent of all Business-to-Business (**http://www.ecommercetimes.com/news/articles/991222-5.shtml**) purchases will be made online by 2003. The figures, which are based on an expected growth rate of 33 percent per year from 1998 to 2003, indicate that the online market will be worth as much as $2.8 trillion (US$) in transaction value.

North America currently dominates the global Business-to-Business E-Commerce picture, with a $700 billion market, twice the size of the non-North American nations combined. "North America will likely retain its significant lead over the next few years, but the global dynamics of Business-to-Business E-Commerce will shift," BCG predicts.

Just as acceleration is expected in Western European consumer E-Commerce, the same can be said for Business-to-Business purchasing, which lags eighteen months behind North America. New investments and initiatives in Western Europe will close that gap over the next few years, although change in Asia and Latin America can be expected to take a bit longer. Nevertheless, the North American market will still come close to doubling the rest of the world. By 2003, North America will reach $3 trillion in Business-to-Business E-Commerce, while the rest of the world will contribute about $1.8 trillion.

QUESTIONS

1. Who will drive E-Commerce growth over the next few years?
(**http://www.ecommercetimes.com/news/articles2000/000712-7.shtml**)

2. Where will mobile E-Commerce work best?
(**http://www.ecmgt.com/Jun2000/management.perspective.htm**)

3. Describe the three forms of Digital TV user access.
(**http://www.ecommercetimes.com/news/articles2000/000320-1.shtml**)

About the Author

Brian Satterlee, who holds doctorates in Education and in Business Administration, is active in three fields: individual, corporate and education.

- In the corporate field, he serves as an organizational consultant.
- In the field of education, he has served as full professor of Business Administration at three private, liberal arts universities. He has been teaching college-level courses continuously since 1980.
- Finally, he serves as a professional coach, helping people worldwide achieve their dreams and goals.

Prior positions included School of Business Dean, Dean of Graduate and Professional Studies, Dean of Adult Education, Business Department Chairperson, Director of Technical Education, and Division of Engineering Technology Chairperson.

He has served on many reaffirmation of accreditation teams for the Southern Association of Colleges and Schools, and has experiences consulting with organizations in the Caribbean Basin concerning program review, evaluation, and strategic planning. He has published nationally within his discipline, and has presented papers at professional conferences.

Dr. Satterlee has consulted with numerous organizations on topics related to strategic management and planning, organizational development, human resources development, distance learning initiatives, leadership development, and the development and evaluation of educational programs and services.

Brian Satterlee may be reached at **http://www.maxpages.com/catalyst**

Appendix

ANSWERS TO END OF CHAPTER QUESTIONS

Chapter 1 DEFINING E-COMMERCE

1. For E-Commerce to thrive, certain critical characteristics must be in place. These include a stable government, a secure financial environment, a competitive marketplace, open systems and standards, high-speed/competitively offered communications, and a climate that fosters innovation.

2. SET: Secure Electronic Transactions is a software code system that is used by the credit card companies to protect their clients. This code is standard for both Visa and Master Charge. OPS: Open Profiling Standards: General information concerning buying habits and other purchasing behaviors that are standardized and can be shared, if desired, to ensure the consumer has the benefits of potential Internet sales, without harassment of e-junk mail advertisements. SSL: Secure Sockets Layer: This coding is created using public key encryption and protects data as it travels over the Internet. Initially developed by Netscape to protect its users who used the Netscape browser. These computer software code systems assist the user to protect their clients' information from being exposed to potential hackers of their websites and digital networks.

3. As for Business-to-Business systems, the issues are less emotional but still serious. Businesses do not yet have good models for setting up their E-Commerce sites, and they have trouble sharing the orders and information

collected online with the rest of their business applications. Many companies continue to grapple with the idea of sharing proprietary business information with customers and suppliers—an important component of many Business-to-Business E-Commerce systems.

Chapter 2: GLOBAL IMPLICATIONS

1. Customs and taxation, electronic payments

2. Fairness and truthfulness in advertising, labeling and other disclosure requirements, refund mechanisms in case of cancelled orders, means of qualifying merchants in terms of the above.

3. The seven tips for globalization are as follows.
   1.Evaluate and prioritize markets before charging ahead. Apply sound business practices. Make sure a potential customer base exists and that benefits outweigh costs.

   2. Get signoff from the top. Without a mandate from upper management, adequate budget and resources may not be allocated.

   3. Partner, partner, partner. Collaborate with vendors, bring in consultants, or hire nationals—whatever it takes to partner with locals. This is an effective way to gain insights, connections, and credibility into the new territory being targeting.

   4. Consider the technical capabilities of the area. Be aware of bandwidth limitations and access charges. Hefty access fees and unique technologies that crash systems won't encourage customers to return to the site.

5. Localize content and keep it fresh. From adhering to the subtle nuances of local language to selecting and presenting products, keep customers' cultures in mind. Avoid making them feel like foreigners or second- class citizens at "their own" site.

6. Act wisely but quickly. A firm may be the" new kid on the block" but it is probably not the only one. Leverage Internet expertise as a foreign-based company, but don't underestimate foreign competitors lead in terms of presence, credibility, and savvy cultural insights.

7. You're not in Kansas anymore. Literally. Above all, respect other cultures. Do not assume anything. Adhere to the overused but wise mandate: When in Rome, do like the Romans.

Chapter 3: LEGAL IMPLICATIONS

1. When doing business on the Internet, one is automatically an international organization and subject to the laws of all nations in which one transacts.

2. Remain as-is, requiring consumers to pay taxes on in-state purchases, allowing them to avoid taxes on most out-of-state purchases. Regularize the status quo by banning sales taxes for all Internet purchases. Set up a system that will allow states to collect use taxes on out-of-state purchases. Eliminate the sales tax for all purchases, online and offline, and use other forms of taxation to make up for the lost revenue.

3. FOR: The Internet is a relatively new medium and E-Commerce is vastly different than any other forms of business. Laws regarding antitrust, copyrights, contracts, and privacy were all developed before the Internet and E-Commerce. Now business transactions occur at fast speeds and

often consumers and sellers have no idea who the other part is, nor will they. Technology is changing quickly and it is impossible for laws that were passed before E-Commerce was even though of to apply to this new media.

AGAINST: No matter how one views E-Commerce, it is still commerce. Vendors attempt to find buyers and buyers attempt to find vendors. The laws that were enacted in the past to regulate commerce still apply. When government has attempted to pass laws that deal solely with the Internet and E-commerce, these laws have been poorly defined. The rationale: there is no difference between transactions that occur with E-Commerce and transactions that occur through typical means.

Chapter 4: ECONOMIC IMPACTS

1. Quality features, large game selections, sports books bets, foreign language sites, good payout rates and timely payouts.

2. The prices were determined neither by science nor art—it was a game played without rules. Several times before the official date of the offering, the initial price was raised. Hype was still important in the initial stock price.

3. Most customer complaints center on the time it takes to make the purchase, receive a response from customer service, or to receive the products that have been ordered. The E-tailers that survive will likely be those that streamline websites for fast, easy navigation and that can ensure rapid or—in some cases—same-day delivery. Ultimately, in an industry whose calling card is convenience, minutes and hours may soon spell the difference between success and failure.

Chapter 5: CONSUMER MOTIVATION FOR E-COMMERCE USE

1. Maintain a link to your ordering information on each page of the site. If more than five products are offered, make sure a shopping cart is available on the website. Do not expect prospects to write down names of products and buying codes. Offer prospects the opportunity to order by secure server, telephone, fax and snail-mail. Allow wire transfers and payment by Western Union.

2. Infrastructure, Applications, Intermediary, and Commerce

3. The Wharton Virtual Test Market tracked more than 23,000 panelists from 1997 through 2000, including preliminary results from 791 participants who have been on the panel for all three years. These same-sample studies have shown a slowing in spending by the same individuals over time. Other studies note the dropout phenomenon and the slower growth of consumers coming online. *Cyber Dialogue* reported that 27 million U.S. adults gave up using the Internet in 2000. The Wharton results indicate that those forecasts may need to be revised downward. Based on the Virtual Test Market survey, Wharton research estimate current levels of consumer online spending at about $29.2 billion and project that that Internet retail sales will climb to $133 billion by January 2004.

Chapter 6: SECURITY FOR CONSUMERS

1. Many experts believe that online transactions are safer than transactions completed at a retail store because there is less human element in an online transaction. A great deal of the credit card fraud that occurs is caused by retail employees that handle the cards. E-Commerce transactions make this impossible by encrypting the numbers on company servers. Another reason that experts argue E-Commerce is safer is that

there is no "brick-and-mortar" store that can be robbed, burned, or ransacked.

2. Any five of the following:
Know the person or organization you are dealing with.
Avoid Spam.
Know the seller by more than a website - the address and phone.
Know if the seller is someone outside the United States.
Know if the seller has experience selling the item.
Know if the company is an authorized seller?
Be leery of shopping for the lowest price.
Know if the seller is still selling online.

3. Under the opt-in model, consumers would be greeted with a pop-up screen upon each visit to a site, prompting them to give or withhold permission with respect to each item of personal information the site wants to collect. Many members of the industry oppose this option, saying that it would inconvenience consumers and tend to make them flee a site. Critics of the opt-in solution are promoting the opt-out method, which allows consumers to withhold permission to collect their personal information by clicking on an easy-to-find screen. Though Internet businesses prefer it, others oppose the opt-out model because it requires consumers to take the initiative in protecting their privacy.

Chapter 7: SECURITY SYSTEMS FOR E-COMMERCE

1. Anyone who has ever tried to download a software program from the Internet has encountered at least licensing agreements users must "sign." The intent of those "contracts" is to make people believe they are signing away their rights to any potential compensation should the software prove faulty.

2. Truste, was an organization developed to monitor Internet privacy issues and discover violators of a strict policy. Firms such as American Online, Excite@home and Microsoft are all members of this organization and have since removed the offending programs from their web browsers. Ironically, Truste only used the software, **thecouter.com**, for two weeks before being caught by a hacking organization, **Interhack.com**. In a statement, the organization said it wanted to be able to track which pages on its site were getting the most visitors and chose the product specifically because it believed no personal data would be gathered. Interhack, however, found that theCounter.com has the technical ability to engage in "detailed profiling" through use of cookies and a cache bug known as "meantime."

3. Both answers are correct in that all systems are designed to prevent anyone from obtaining unauthorized access. However, with the a large amount of time, money and resources there is always an opportunity to gain unauthorized access. Encrypted technology are mechanisms network programmers use to prevent unauthorized access, but these systems also have decoding sequences, and many times disgruntled employees can provide hackers with this information. Attackers have tools such as "packet sniffers" that give them the ability to monitor a computer network, accessing confidential e-mails, account names, passwords and credit card information.

Chapter 8: DISTRIBUTION

1. It either inflates the cost of customer acquisition, or is translated to the customer through the ticket price on each item.

2. Regardless of how difficult it has been for some manufacturers to sell online, there may be ways to sell directly to customers without offending

suppliers in the distribution channel. Some manufacturers sell a product line that is only sold on the Internet. That way, retailers do not find them in direct competition. Others with well-known brand names may take advantage of the power of online sales by selling products under a different brand name. Still, manufacturers are likely to tread cautiously in moving their operations online.

3. How large is your inventory?
   What is your inventory?
   How much can you budget for fulfillment?
   How fast do you need to get your products delivered?
   Do you need customer, promotional, or marketing, support?
   Is your business data system compatible with that of the fulfillment services?

Chapter 9: PROMOTION AND MARKETING

1. (a) Establish outsourced call centers that can deal quickly and efficiently with queries that cannot be dealt with over the Web; (b) Provide customers with a foolproof mechanism for returns—a key element to the value chain that cannot be provided over the Internet; (c) Invest in the physical infrastructure to ensure that delivery and storage facilities can meet customer demand; (d) Invest in the data center and consider outsourcing its management to a data monitoring specialist; and (e) Make sure the complete experience, from the moment a customer enters the Web site through fulfillment, delivery and return, is as easy as possible from the customer viewpoint.

2. Speed to market has been generally considered the key factor to online success,

3. Concern among Internet users and advocacy groups that personal data will be exploited by marketers has led most merchants to use such information only with great caution. Meanwhile, many Web merchants have found themselves confronting more pressing operational tasks, like setting up the systems for credit-card transactions or inventory management. In many cases, merchants have not installed the right technology for making sense of the flood of raw data generated by user traffic on their sites, or hired someone to analyze that data. It's a matter of finding the time to analyze all of the information gathered. E-Commerce retailers must also determine if using the information is an invasion of privacy or a service to the consumer.

Chapter 10: CHANNELS TO MARKET

1. Retail, motor vehicles, shipping, industrial equipment, high tech and government tend to gain most.

2. The travel, computer hardware and software, financial brokerage, and collectible categories claimed 70 percent of the E-Commerce market.

3. B2B transactions offer the possibility of cost cutting advantages in price, which in turn can reduce bottom line costs for a company. However, these transactions lose the personal relationships that have been built on trust and loyalty. Some businesses are more interested in reliability, quality and excellent service from vendors who have proven their worth over the long run, and they will not be lured to the anonymous Internet merely on the chance that they can save a few pennies on the dollar. The dilemma is whether or not B2B can provide the cost reductions necessary to provide strong enough reason to leave current vendors with whom the company has developed a strong relationship.

Chapter 11: STRATEGIC PLANNING FOR DIRECT CONSUMER E-COMMERCE

1. Online shoppers pushed consumer-based E-Commerce revenues to almost $8 billion in 1998, according to Forrester Research. And analysts are united in the belief that those numbers will continue to grow at a brisk pace for years to come. There are several reasons:

- Choice. Shoppers are no longer limited by how far they can drive. And "shopping bots" are now helping to automate and personalize the online shopping experience, providing exactly what the consumer wants at the lowest possible price.
- Convenience. Online stores never close.
- Better consumer information. The proliferation of online consumer information, such as the dealer costs of new automobiles and self-published consumer comments and reviews, has heightened consumer savvy.

2. Attitudes/beliefs are quicker and easier to test. Dialogues, with consumers, are easier to maintain, and opinions, are easier to record. Costs are minimal to electronically capture these subjects. Visitors to a website are easily tracked regarding number of visits, length of visit, and depth of site penetration, using-measurement software. As a result, traditional media are regarded as read-only type mechanisms, pushing one-way information upon the customer. With the advent of electronic commerce, the interaction is one-to-one, in real-time.

3. The idea of Electronic Commerce isn't brand new. Ideas such as computer-based shopping and electronic data interchange have been under development for years. But Internet-based E-Commerce technologies are now truly revolutionizing business practices around the globe. Consumer E-Commerce receives most of the hoopla, but Business-to-Business E-Commerce currently earns most of the revenues

and productivity gains. Michigan's information technology business sector faces several barriers, most notably worker retention and recruitment and image problems. Despite barriers, Michigan companies large and small are developing a bustling E-Commerce business sector. Auto companies are developing leading edge Business-to-Business and consumer applications. Retailers large and small are competing in the online marketplace. And technical firms headquartered in Michigan are exporting E-Commerce talent and technology to many other states and regions of the world. Taxation issues will likely impact Michigan's E-Commerce business sector in coming years. On the one hand, legislative proposals may ease tax burdens on high-tech companies. On the other, Internet taxation might stunt E-Commerce growth as Michigan, like all states, seeks to remedy a major tax revenue drain caused by the growth of E-Commerce across state boundaries.

Chapter 12: INTERNET STRATEGY AND IMPLEMENTATION

1. Shipping services linked to E-Commerce should provide a complete pick, pack and shipping service, coupled with shipping options such as same day, as ordered and international shipping options. In addition they should offer various value to cost shipping speed options and provide both receiving and warehousing services.

2. The reality is that while the Internet provides a powerful platform for aggregation and matching, this development becomes moot if the Internet cannot be levered to also drive scale on the back end as well. As a result, one of the fundamental impacts of the Internet on business-and the most significant opportunity for solutions providers-will be in optimizing the flow of information, resources, materials, and services from suppliers to manufacturers, to end customers. This flow is the essence of Web-enabled supply chain management applications-e-supply Web solutions.

3. A number of dominant industries have jumped on to the Internet bandwagon, including IT industry, publishers, retailers, banks and financial institutions, airlines and others. The following list highlights a few of the thousands of examples:

- Airlines - hundreds of airlines throughout the globe have created Web sites, and a number are not only taking queries, but are actually receiving orders for tickets;
- Banks - a site provided by IFBG Gottingen lists some 140 European banks on the Web from 26 countries;
- Media & Publishing - many publishing houses have developed Web versions of traditional print media, and entirely new e-zines;
- Retail - perhaps one of the most famous examples of marketing on the Web comes from Van den Bergh Foods - otherwise known as Ragu (http://eat.com). Hundreds of recipes and an online soap opera fill this site! Interflora is another example of adding value to existing services, Interflora was only open to small niche regional locations on the east and west coast.

Chapter 13: ELECTRONIC PAYMENT

1. Internet Billing Co., Ltd. (ibill) is a premier provider of transaction processing and services that enable Web merchants to accept and process real-time payments for goods and services purchased over the Internet and manage back-office functions using ibill's Commerce Management Interfaces (CMIs). The benefits to the end users is that the encrypted technology allows users to make real time payments that protect both the user and the merchant.

2. The growing importance of electronic commerce has resulted in the introduction of a variety of different and incompatible payment systems. For business application developers, this variety implies the need to under-

stand the details of different systems, to adapt the code as soon as new payment systems are introduced, and also to provide a way of picking a suitable payment instrument for every transaction

3. Any of the following:

- Performing real-time online transactions from your Web site with WebLink.
- Performing real-time manual transactions with Virtual Terminal.
- Processing periodic billing through the batch upload function.
- Protecting against fraudulent transactions with the Address Verification Service (AVS).
- Taking advantage of complete online reporting capabilities.
- Accessing sales data from any computer in the world with Internet access and a Web browser.
- Offering electronic check payment options with eCheck.Net.
- Eliminating the need for additional hardware or software.
- Being compatible with any hardware and operating platform.
- Eliminating costly software upgrades and updates.
- Supporting an unlimited number of users simultaneously.
- Automatically settling transactions daily.
- Offering tech support via an email menu item - with a 24-hour response time.

Chapter 14: AUCTION TECHNOLOGY

1. Fixed closing or open ending bidding, Real time or bid-ask bidding, Do it yourself vs. Third party provider, State and local regulations and laws concerning selling goods, such as alcohol and tobacco.

2. Suppliers should have an accurate in-depth knowledge of their costs, because as the E-Commerce model continues to grow, suppliers with the lowest costs will be the ultimate winners.

3. Any of the following:
- Do not start bidding until you've done some research on the items you're looking for
- Get your bid in early
- Don't bid too high
- Talk online with other buyers to find out about trends, and get an idea of which objects could sell well in the future
- Make sure you're bidding with a powerful computer so you can respond quickly if you get a rival bid
- Try shopping at the overseas sites of UK-based companies and see if you can find any bargains
- Investigate the categories that are available online - you might find you're sitting on something valuable
- Carefully consider all free insurance offers to cover anything you buy online
- Investigate any special secure payment services provided by the online auction houses
- If you're planning to use a robot to bid for you in an online auction, remember to set sensible bidding limits

Chapter 15: FUTURE IMPLICATIONS

1. E-Commerce growth will be driven by new users and buyers over the next few years.

2. Mobile E-Commerce will work best in areas where it can emphasize convenience, personalization, and location.

3. The three types of use of digital TV are single mode, simultaneous mode and pause mode. Single Mode allows the TV viewer to switch between the television program and the interactive application. When the viewer finishes the interactive activity, he or she returns to regular viewing. In simultaneous mode the viewer inserts the interactive application into a picture-in-picture (PIP) window on the television screen and is able to interact while continuing to watch the program. The pause mode records television programs to a hard disk, thereby allowing viewers to pause the program in order to use the full screen to take advantage of the interactive service. When the interaction is over, viewers can continue the program at the point where it was paused.